William Henry Furness, Phil., Pe., First Cong. Unitarian Church

Exercises at the Meeting of the First Congregational Unitarian Society

January 12, 1875 - together with the discourse delivered by Rev. W.H. Furness, D.D., Sunday, Jan. 10, 1875

William Henry Furness, Phil., Pe., First Cong. Unitarian Church

Exercises at the Meeting of the First Congregational Unitarian Society
January 12, 1875 - together with the discourse delivered by Rev. W.H. Furness, D.D., Sunday, Jan. 10, 1875

ISBN/EAN: 9783337819415

Printed in Europe, USA, Canada, Australia, Japan

Cover: Foto ©Lupo / pixelio.de

More available books at **www.hansebooks.com**

Exercises

AT THE MEETING OF

THE

First Congregational Unitarian Society,

January 12, 1875,

TOGETHER WITH THE DISCOURSE DELIVERED BY

REV. W. H. FURNESS, D.D.,

Sunday, Jan. 10, 1875,

On the Occasion of the Fiftieth Anniversary of his Ordination,

January 12, 1825.

PHILADELPHIA:
SHERMAN & CO., PRINTERS.
1875.

First Congregational Unitarian Society.

On November 3d, 1874, the Trustees of the First Congregational Unitarian Church of Philadelphia issued the following notice to the members of the parish:

FIRST CONGREGATIONAL SOCIETY OF UNITARIAN CHRISTIANS.

PHILADELPHIA, November 3d, 1874.

A meeting of the members of this Society will be held at the Church on Monday, the 9th inst., at 8 P. M., to devise an appropriate plan for celebrating the completion of the fiftieth year of Dr. FURNESS' pastorate.

As his half century of faithful and distinguished service calls for fitting commemoration, and as the members of this Church must rejoice at an opportunity of giving expression to their love, admiration, and respect for him, a meeting that concerns such an object will commend itself, and prove of interest to every one, so that the bare announcement of it, it is deemed, will be sufficient to insure a full attendance of the parishioners.

By direction of the Trustees,

CHARLES H. COXE,
Secretary.

In pursuance of this notice, the members of the Society held a meeting in the Church on the evening of November 9th, 1874, to consider the subject proposed.

The meeting was organized with Mr. B. H. Bartol as Chairman, and Mr. Charles H. Coxe as Secretary.

After stating the object of the meeting, the Chairman called for the opinion of the Society. It was voted that a committee of nine be appointed, who should, together with the Trustees of the Church, constitute a committee to take entire charge of the celebration of Dr. Furness' Fiftieth Anniversary as Pastor of the Church; should have full power to add to their number, and make such arrangements as might seem to them suitable to the occasion.

The Chair appointed on this Committee,

Mrs. R. S. Sturgis,	Miss Duhring,
Mrs. J. E. Raymond,	Mr. John Sartain,
Miss Clark,	Mr. B. H. Moore,
Miss Roberts,	Mr. David Brewer,

And at the request of the meeting, Mr. B. H. Bartol, the Chairman, was added.

On November 14th, 1874, at 8 o'clock P. M., the Committee appointed by the Society held a meeting at the residence of Mr. B. H. Bartol, to make arrangements for the fiftieth anniversary of Dr. Furness' pastorate.

The Committee consisted of the following persons:

Trustees.

Mr. Henry Winsor,	Mr. Lucius H. Warren,
Mr. John Sellers, Jr ,	Mr. Joseph E. Raymond,
Mr. Enoch Lewis,	Mr. D. E. Furness,

Mr. Charles H. Coxe.

Appointed by the Society.

Mrs. R. S. Sturgis, Miss Duhring,
Mrs. J. E. Raymond, Mr. John Sartain,
Miss Clark, Mr. B. H. Moore,
Miss Roberts, Mr. David Brewer,
Mr. B. H. Bartol.

Mr. Winsor was chosen Chairman, and Mr. Charles H. Coxe, Secretary.

It was voted, that on the evening of January 12th, 1875, there should be a commemorative service in the Church, and ministers from other cities should be invited to be present.

The Chair appointed as the Committee on Invitations,

Mr. L. H. Warren, Mr. Enoch Lewis,
Mr. B. H. Bartol, Mr. David Brewer,
Mr. B. H. Moore,
And at the request of the Committee
Mr. Henry Winsor.

It was also voted, that the Church should be handsomely and appropriately decorated on that occasion.

The Chair appointed as the Committee on Decorations,

Mr. Joseph E. Raymond, Mrs. R. S. Sturgis,
Mr. L. H. Warren, Miss Clark,
Miss Roberts, Miss Duhring.

It was also voted, that the Choir on that occasion should be increased, if it should be deemed expedient by the Musical Committee of the Church.

It was further voted, that a marble bust of Dr. Furness should be obtained, and placed in the Church.

Also, that gold and bronze medals should be struck off, commemorative of the fiftieth anniversary of the pastorate of Dr. Furness,

And also, that a suitable and handsome present should be given to Dr. Furness, in the name of the Society, as a token of their affection and gratitude.

Also, that photographs of the Church should be taken as it appeared on the day of the anniversary.

The Chair appointed as the Committee on Fine Arts,

  Mr. John Sartain, Mr. B. H. Moore,
    Mr. Henry Winsor.

It was also voted, that the exercises at the ordination of Dr. Furness should be reprinted, and that the anniversary sermon and the exercises at the commemorative service should be printed in pamphlet form.

The Chair appointed as the Committee on Publication,

  Mr. Dawes E. Furness.

And as the Committee on Finance,

  Mr. B. H. Bartol, Mr. Enoch Lewis,
    Mr. Charles H. Coxe.

On Sunday, January 10th, 1875, Rev. Dr. Furness preached his fiftieth anniversary sermon.

The following account is taken from the *Christian Register* of that week:

"Yesterday was as perfect a winter day as can be imagined, cool, clear, and bright. The Unitarian church was filled before the hour of worship with an eager and deeply interested throng. All the pews were occupied, and the aisles and the space around the pulpit were filled with chairs. The church was beautifully decorated with laurel wreaths, and in front of the pulpit the floral array was very rich yet very chaste. On the wall in the rear of the pulpit was an exquisite ivy cross. Among the festoons which overhung the pulpit were the figures '1825' and '1875' in white and red flowers.

"Dr. Furness seemed to be in excellent health, and took his part in the rare and touching semi-centennial service without any apparent exhaustion. After a brief recital and paraphrase of appropriate passages of Scripture, he read with great beauty and tenderness the hymn beginning, 'While Thee I seek, protecting Power,' and after a prayer full of love, trust, and gratitude, he read from the twentieth chapter of the Book of Acts, beginning at the seventeenth verse. Then the congregation sang Lyte's beautiful hymn, 'Abide with me! fast falls the eventide,' etc. The discourse had no text, excepting the impressive occasion itself. There was less of narration of interesting incidents than in previous anniversary sermons, yet the half century was reviewed in a simple and masterly way. The preacher's manner was quite subdued until he reached his studies of the life of Jesus, when his face became radiant, his tones fuller and firmer, and his gestures frequent. The allusions to other denominations and to the anti-slavery struggle were exceedingly fair and magnanimous. The people gave rapt attention, and there was evident regret when the sermon closed.

"The singing by a double quartette choir was highly creditable. Mr. Ames' church at Germantown was closed, and pastor and people came to express their sympathy with Dr. Furness' society, and to enjoy the uplifting service. Dr. Martineau's new hymn-book was used, Dr. Furness having presented his parishioners with a sufficient number of copies to supply all the pews."

DISCOURSE

DELIVERED

SUNDAY JANUARY 10, 1875,

ON THE OCCASION OF THE

FIFTIETH ANNIVERSARY

OF HIS

ORDINATION, JANUARY 12, 1825, AS THE PASTOR

OF THE

First Congregational Unitarian Church

BY

W. H. FURNESS D.D.

DISCOURSE

It is in vain, dear friends, that I have tried to set in order the thoughts that come crowding upon me as the fiftieth year of my service in this place draws to a close. I cannot tell what direction they will take. But for the uncertainty of life, I might have reserved for this occasion the Recollections in which I indulged on the last two anniversaries of my Ordination. All I told you then and countless other memories come vividly to mind and heart now. They almost hush me into silence, so hopeless is the endeavor to give them utterance. I must needs talk about myself. How can it be avoided on an occasion like this? I trust in the kind indulgence on your part which has never failed me in all these years. If I should prove only garrulous, you will not forget that I have passed the allotted boundary and am now one of the borrowers from eternity; although it hardly becomes me to make claim to the privileges of age in a community where dwells one, known and revered of all, who has entered his ninety-sixth year, and is not yet old.

First of all, most humbly and heartily do I acknowledge and adore the good Providence that, for no deserving of mine, has blest me so bountifully and so long, and given me such a dear home among you. What friends, kith and kin to me, have always surrounded me! At the first here were my fathers—I have followed them all to the grave. And now, behold! my brothers, my sisters, my children. What a gift of God the filial, the fraternal, the parental trust which I have been encouraged to cherish! It has been my chiefest treasure, the dearest sign of Heaven's grace, my support, my well-spring of life.

During my ministry I have received from you, from time to time, not a few unlooked-for, substantial tokens of your kind thoughts for me. They shall never be forgotten. But it is not the remembrance of any special proofs of your regard that now moves me, but the hearty faith in your good-will upon which you have always given me reason to rely. This has been my crowning privilege.

Even when differences have arisen between us, my trust in your personal regard has never been allowed to be shaken. Were there exceptions, they are as good as forgotten now. Even those who have taken such offence at my words that they withdrew from the church, still gave me assurance of their friendship. There used to be times of painful excitement among us, you remember, when I was helpless to resist the impulse to plead for the oppressed. I can never forget how cheered I was by one friend, still living, but not now dwelling in this city, who came to me and said that he had at the first disapproved of my course, but that he was then in full sympathy with me, and that, as to the church's being broken up, as was predicted, if I persisted in speaking for the slave, that should not be, if a contribution to its support from him (and he named a most liberal sum), could prevent it. Of course I never thought of availing myself of his generous aid, or of permitting the contingency to occur that would make it needful. If it had come to that pass I should have felt myself bound to withdraw.

You will not think that I offend against propriety in mentioning such a private experience when you consider what an encouragement it was, what a joy to know that I had such friends.

Indeed, I would not refer now to those painful times at all, could I not in all honesty say that I look back upon them with pride, not on my own account, oh no! but on yours, dear friends, on yours. How I feared and trembled, and with what a faltering voice did I deliver the messages of truth that came to me! You resisted them too. I tried to hold my tongue and you to shut your ears. I would fain have run away and hid myself from the summons of Humanity. But I could not do that. I could not resign my position without putting you in a false one, in a position which I did not believe you were willing to take. And you were not willing. This church, I say it proudly, never committed itself to the Wrong. You never took any action on that side. On the contrary, when, in the midst of that agitation, I was honored with an invitation elsewhere, and you had the opportunity of relief by my being transferred to another church, you asserted, at a very full meeting, with decisive unanimity, your fidelity to the freedom of the pulpit. And now it may be written in the annals of this Church that in that trying time, it stood fast on the ground of Christian Liberty, and its minister had the honor of being its representative.

While I gratefully acknowledge the friendship which has been my special blessing for half a century, I gladly repeat what I have said on former anniversaries of my ministry, that the kindness I have received has not come from you alone. How little has there been in all this time to remind me that we of this Church bear an obnoxious name! How many are there who are not of this little fold, but of other denominations, who have made me feel that they belonged to me! O friends, it is not all bearing the same religious name, but all bearing different religious names and yet each respecting in others the right of every one to think for himself,—this it is that illustrates most impressively the broad spirit of our common Christianity. I had rather see this fact manifest than a hundred churches agreeing exactly with me in opinion.

I preached my first sermon in the fall of 1823, in Watertown, Massachusetts. And then, for a few months, I preached as a candidate for settlement in Churches in Boston and its vicinity needing pastors. Kind and flattering things were said to me of my ministrations, but I put little faith in them, as they came from the many relatives and friends that I and mine had in that quarter, and their judgment was biased by regard for me and mine. I was strengthened in my distrust when friends, fellow-students, and fellow-candidates, were preferred before me. I never envied them their success. I felt not the slightest mortification, such a hearty dread had I of being settled in Boston, whose church-goers had in those days the reputation of being terribly critical, and rhetoric then and there was almost a religion. I felt myself utterly unequal to that position. All my day-dreams had been of the country, of some village church.

In May, 1824, I gladly availed myself of the opportunity that was offered me of spending three months in Baltimore as an assistant of Mr Greenwood, afterwards pastor of the Stone Chapel, Boston. Before I left Baltimore, the last of July of that year, I received a letter from this city, inviting me to stop on my way home and preach a few Sundays in the little church here. I accepted the invitation as in duty bound, but rather reluctantly, as I had never before been so long and so far away from home, and I was homesick. I spent the month of August here. I do not recollect that I had any thought of being a candidate for this pulpit. Such had been my experience, my ill success,—I do not wonder at it now,—that I was surprised and gratified when, upon the eve of my departure, I was waited upon by a committee of four or five,—I have had a suspicion since, so few were the members of this Church then, that this committee comprised nearly the whole Church meeting from which they came,—and they cordially invited me to return and become their pastor. As I had come here a perfect stranger, and there were no prepossessions in my favor, I could not but have at the very first a gratifying confidence in this invitation. Although I asked time for consideration, I responded at once in my heart to the kindness shown to me. Thus the aspirant to a country parish was led to this great city.

The three hundred miles and more that separate Philadelphia from my native Boston were a great deal longer then than they are now. It took then at least two days and a half to go from one to the other. A minister of our denomination in Boston and its neighborhood had then a great help in the custom then and there prevalent of a frequent exchange of pulpits. One seldom occupied his own pulpit more than half of the time. But this church in Philadelphia was an outpost, and the lightening of the labor by exchanges was not to be looked for. There was no one to exchange with nearer than William Ware, pastor of the church in New York. The place to be filled here looked lonely and formidable. I accepted, however, the lead of circumstances, moved by the confidence with which the hospitable members of this church inspired me. I was drawn to this part of the vineyard by their readiness to welcome me.

My ordination was delayed some months by the difficulty of obtaining ministers to come and take part in it. It was a journey then. The days had only just gone by when our pious New England fathers who made it had prayers offered up in their churches for the protection of

Heaven (or rather in their meeting-houses, as all places of worship except the Catholic and Episcopal were called; we never talked of going to church, we went to meeting). Ordinations have ceased to be the solemn occasions they were then. Then they were sacramental in their signification, like marriage. As our liberal faith was then everywhere spoken against, it was thought necessary that my ordination should be conducted as impressively as possible. It is pleasant now to remember that with the two Wares, Henry Ware, Jr, and William, and Dr Gannett, came one of the fathers, far advanced in years, the venerable Dr Bancroft, of Worcester, Mass., the honored father of a distinguished son, to partake in the exercises of the occasion. They are all gone now.

This Church had its beginning in 1796, when seven persons, nearly all from the old country, shortly increased to fourteen, with their families, agreed, at the suggestion of Dr Priestley, who came to this country in 1794, to meet every Sunday and take turns as readers of printed sermons and prayers of the Liberal Faith. These meetings were occasionally interrupted by the yellow fever, by which Philadelphia was then visited almost every year, but they were never wholly given up.

In 1813 the small brick building was built in which I first preached, and which stood on the southwest corner of the present lot, directly on the street. A charter was then obtained under the title of "The First Society of Unitarian Christians." So obnoxious then was the Unitarian name that the most advanced men of our faith in Boston, the fountain-head of American Unitarianism, remonstrated with the fathers of this church, and counselled them to abstain from the use of so unpopular a designation. But our founders, being Unitarians from Old England and not from New, and consequently warm admirers, and some of them personal friends, of Dr Priestley, whose autograph was on their records as one of their members, felt themselves only honored in bearing with him the opprobrium of the Unitarian name. The title of our Church was afterwards changed to its present denomination, to bring it nominally into accord with our brethren in New England. In 1828 this building took the place of the first.

It was about ten years before I came here that the Trinitarian and Unitarian controversy began. One of its earliest forms appeared in published letters in 1815 between Dr Channing, the pastor of the Federal Street Church in Boston, and Dr Samuel Worcester, an able orthodox minister of Salem, Mass. In 1819 Dr Channing preached a sermon at the ordination of Mr Sparks in Baltimore, which was then and ever will be regarded as an eloquent and felicitous statement of the views of the liberally disposed of that day. It commanded great attention far and wide, and gave occasion to a very able, learned, and courteous controversy between Dr Woods and Mr Stuart, professors in the Orthodox Theological School in Andover, Mass., on the one side, and Professors Henry Ware, Sr, and Andrews Norton, of the Cambridge Theological School on the other. The controversy spread mostly in Massachusetts. In the small towns where there had been only one church, there speedily appeared two. Families were divided, not without heats and coolnesses, to the hurt of Christian fellowship. As a general rule, fathers took the liberal side, mothers the orthodox.

When I came here in 1825, the first excitement of the controversy had somewhat subsided. It had lost its first keen interest. It was growing rather wearisome. It had snowed tracts, Trinitarian and Unitarian, over the land. Accordingly, although I was a warm partisan, full of confidence in the rational and scriptural superiority of the Unitarian faith, I did not feel moved to preach doctrinal sermons. And, furthermore, as I was on my way hither in the mail coach, in company with my friends, ministers and delegates from Boston and New York, I was greatly impressed by a remark made by one of my elders to the effect that people were bound to their several churches, not by the force of reason and the results of religious inquiry, but by mere use and wont and affection.

Of the truth of this remark, by the way, I had a striking instance some years ago. One of our fellow-citizens, now deceased, an intelligent, respectable man, a devoted member of one of our Presbyterian churches, used to come to me to borrow Theodore Parker's writings, in which he took great pleasure. But he said he never dreamed of withdrawing from his Church. As Richter says, his Church was his mother. You could not have weaned him from her by telling him how many better mothers there were in the world. This truth impressed me greatly, and was a comfort to me in my younger days.

Although I have rarely preached an outright doctrinal discourse, yet I had many interesting experiences in reference to the spread of liberal ideas. I regret that I have not done in my small way what that eminent man, John Quincy Adams, as his Memoirs now in course of publication show he did in his wonderfully thorough way, —kept a diary. Very frequently has it occurred that persons have come to me who had chanced to hear a Unitarian sermon, or read a Unitarian book for the first time, and they declared that it expressed their views precisely, and they did not know before that there was anybody in the world of that way of thinking.

Once, many years ago, I received a letter from a stranger in Virginia, bearing a well-known Virginia name. She wrote to tell me that a year before, she was in Philadelphia, and, much against her conscience, had been induced by her husband to enter this church. Although there was nothing of a doctrinal character in the sermon, the effect was to move her when she returned home to study the Scriptures for herself with new care. The result was that she now believed upon their authority that there was only one God, the Father, and that Jesus Christ was a dependent being. There were some texts, however, that she wished to have explained, and therefore she wrote to me. The texts she specified showed that she could not have met with any of our publications, for, had she done so, she would certainly have found the explanations she desired. Of course I did what I could to supply her wants.

I think this incident would have passed away from my mind or been only dimly remembered if, twenty-five years afterwards, and after the war of the Rebellion, I had not received another letter from the same person. In it she referred to our correspondence of five-and-twenty years before, and said that she wrote now in behalf of some suffering people, formerly her servants (slaves, I presume). Through the kindness of Mr John Welsh, chairman of a committee that had been chosen by our fellow-citizens for the relief of the Southern people, I was enabled to send her a sum of money. A quantity of clothing was also procured for her from the Freedmen's Relief Association. My Southern friend returned, with her thanks, a very minute account of the disposition she had made of the supplies sent to her. She appeared to have accepted with a Christian grace the changed condition of things in the South. May we not give something of the credit of this gracious behavior to the liberal faith which she had learned to cherish?

It was cases like this that caused me to feel less and less interest in doctrines and religious controversies. I have been learning every day that, much as men differ in religion and numberless other things, they are, after all, more alike than different, and that in our intercourse with our fellow-men it is best to ignore those differences as much as possible, and take for granted that we and they are all of one kind.

And furthermore, in free conversation with educated and intelligent persons of this city, with whom I have become acquainted, I long ago found out that it was not orthodoxy that prevailed; it was not the doctrines of Calvin and the Thirty-nine Articles that were rampant, but that there was a wide-spread scepticism as to the simplest facts of historical Christianity. To persons of this class, numerous, years ago, and not less numerous now, it mattered little whether the Bible taught the Trinity or the Unity of the Divine Nature. The question with them is, whether it be not all a fable.

It was this state of mind that I was continually meeting with that early gave to my humble studies a very definite and positive direction. It was high time, I thought, to look to the very foundations of Christianity, and see to it, not whether the Christian Records, upon which we are all resting, favor the Trinitarian or the Unitarian interpretation of their contents, but whether they have any basis in Fact, and to what that basis amounts. As this seemed to be the fundamental inquiry, so, of all inquiries, it became to me the most interesting.

In studying this question I could not satisfy myself that any external, historical argument, however powerful, in favor of the genuineness and authenticity of the Christian Records, could prove decisive. For even if it were thus proved to demonstration that we have in the Four Gospels the very works, word for word, of the writers whose names they bear, there would still remain untouched the question: How, after all, do we know that these writers, honest and intelligent as they may have been, were not mistaken?

There was only one thing to be done: To examine these writings themselves, and to find out what they really are. With the one single desire to ascertain their true character, that is, whether they be narratives of facts or of fables, or a mingle of both, they were to be studied, and the principles of reason, truth, and probability were to be applied to them just as if they were anonymous fragments recently discovered in some monastery of the East, or dug up from under some ancient ruins.

On the face of them, they are very artlessly constructed. Here was one good reason for believing that, though it might be difficult, it could not be impossible to determine what they are. Since Science can discover in any compound the simples of which it is composed, although present in infinitesimal quantities, surely then it can be ascertained of what these artless works of human hands are made: whether they be the creations of fancy or the productions of truth.

Then, again, as obviously, these primitive Records abound in allusions to times, places, and persons. Here was another ground of hope that the inquiry into their real character would not be in vain. When one is telling a story not founded in fact, he takes good care how he refers to times, and persons, and places, since every such reference is virtually summoning a witness to testify to his credibility.

Encouraged by these considerations, I have now, for forty years and more, given myself to this fundamental inquiry. It has been said that only scholars, far more learned men than I pretend to be, can settle the historical claims of the Four Gospels. But the fact is, the theologians in Germany and elsewhere, profound as their learning is, have busied themselves about the external historical arguments for the truth of the Gospels. They have been given, it has seemed to me, to a quibbling sort of criticism about jots and tittles. But it is not microscopes, but an eye to see with, that is the one thing needed for the elucidation of these Writings.

When we first occupied this building, I read courses of Expository Lectures every Tuesday evening, in a room which was fitted up as a vestry, under the church, for some four or five months in the year, for five seasons. The attendance was never large; some thirty persons perhaps gave me their presence. But my interest in the study came not from my hearers, but from the subject, in which, from that time to this, I have found an increasing delight. Continually new and inimitable marks of truth have been disclosed. Unable to keep to myself what I found so convincing, I have from time to time published the discoveries, or what appeared to me discoveries, that I made. The editions of my little published volumes have never been large. Many persons tell me they have read them. I can reconcile the fact that they have been so much read with their very limited sale only by supposing that the few copies sold have been loaned very extensively. Do not think, friends, that I am making any complaint. As I have just said, my interest in the subject has not depended upon others, either hearers or readers. The subject itself has been my abundant compensation.

To many of my brothers in the ministry I have appeared, I suppose, to be the dupe of my own fancies. What I have offered as sparkling gems of fact have been regarded as made, not found. Some time ago I came across an old letter from my venerated friend, the late Henry Ware, Jr, in which he expostulated with me for wasting myself upon such a barren study as he appears to have regarded the endeavor to ascertain whether this great Christendom be founded on a fable or on the adamant of Fact.

So dependent are we all upon the sympathy of others, that I believe my interest in this pursuit would have abated long ago had it not been that the subject had an overpowering charm in itself, and that one great result of the inquiry, becoming more and more significant at every step, was to bring out in ever clearer light the Godlike Character of the Man of Nazareth. As he has gradually emerged from the thick mists of superstition and theological speculation in which he had so long been hidden from my sight, his Person, as profoundly natural as it was profoundly original, has broken upon me at times as "the light of the knowledge of the glory of God." Not in any alleged miracle, not in any nor in all His works, wonderful and unprecedented as some of them were, not in His words, immortal as is the wisdom that he uttered, but in that reserved fulness of personal power of which His works and words,—His whole overt life gives only a hint, significant, indeed, but only a hint—there, in himself, in what He was, in the native, original power of the Man, the secret of His mighty influence has been laid bare to me. That it is that explains the existence of the wondrous stories of His life. They had to be, and to be just what they are, with all their discrepancies, mistakes, and somewhat of the fabulous that is found in them, born as they were of the irresistible force of His personal truth. And that it is, also, which is the inexhaustible fountain of Inspiration, of Faith, and Love, and Hope, which the Infinite Mercy has opened in the world, and of which men, fainting and perishing in their sins, shall drink, and from within them shall flow rivers of healing and of health.

As I have intimated, friends, there have been times when I have felt somewhat lonely in this study. But some ten years ago a marked change came over the course of religious thought occasioned by the appearance of a Life of Jesus, by an eloquent and learned man in France, who, belonging to the sceptical school, scarcely believing that such a person as Jesus ever had an existence, went to Syria upon a scientific errand, and when there was struck by the evidences that he beheld of the geographical truth of the New Testament. So strong a conviction was born in him of the reality of Jesus that he was moved to write his life. It is true there is little else in the book of Ernest Renan recognized as fact, beyond the actual existence and the great sayings of Jesus. This was something, coming from the quarter it did. And, moreover, with all the doubts which it suggests as to particular incidents in the Gospel histories, its publication has been justified by the effect it had in turning attention to the human side of that great life. It has created a new interest in the Man.

And further, Science, becoming popular, is impressing the general mind so deeply with the idea of the inviolable order of Nature, that it is not to be believed that men will look much longer for the credentials of any person, or of any fact, in his or its departure from that order. Nothing can be recognized as truth that violates the laws of Nature, or rather that does not harmonize with them fully. Deeply impressed with the entire naturalness of Jesus, I believe that the time is at hand when the evidences of His truth, of His divinity, will be sought, not in any preternatural events or theories, but in His full accord with the natural truth of things. As the one Fact, or Person, in whom the highest or deepest in Nature is revealed, He is the central fact, harmonizing all nature.

Never, never, from the first, has it been more important that the personality of Jesus should be appreciated than at the present time. The Darwinian law of Natural

Selection and the Survival of the Fittest is in all men's minds, and in the material, organized world of plants and animals, we are all coming to consider it demonstrated. As an animal, man must be concluded under that law. In the physical world, as Professor Tyndall tells us, " the weakest must go to the wall."

But man is something, a great deal more than an animal. He has an immaterial, moral, intellectual being, for which he has the irresistible testimony of his own consciousness; and as an immaterial being, it is not at the cost of the weak, but it is by helping the weak to live that any individual becomes strong. This, this is the great law of our spiritual nature. The highest, the elect, they whom Nature selects, the fittest to live, are those who are ready to die for others, sacrificing their mortal existence, if need be, to lift up the weakest to their immortal fellowship. In the unchangeable order of things, not only is it not possible for a moral and intellectual being to become great by sacrificing others to his own advancement, his greatness can be secured only by giving himself for them.

Let Science, then, go on pouring light upon the laws and order of the material Universe. But let it stand by its admission that the connection between that and the immaterial world, however intimate, is not only inscrutable, but unthinkable; and reverently recognize, standing there on the threshold of the immaterial world, one Godlike Figure, surrounded by the patriots and martyrs, the great and good of every age and country, holy angels, but high above them all in the perfectness of his Self-abnegation. No one took His life from him; He gave it up freely of himself. And thus is He a special revelation of the law that reigns in the moral world, as surely as the law of natural selection reigns in the physical.

What renders the character of Jesus of still greater interest at this present time is the fact that there are thoughtful and enlightened men who aver that they would fain be rid of Him, since He has been and still is the occasion of so much enslaving error. They might as well, for the same reason, join with Porson and "damn the nature of things," for what has occasioned greater error than the nature of things? It can be got rid of as easily as the Person of Jesus.

For some twenty years or more before the war of the Rebellion, the question which that war settled interested me deeply. But on the last anniversary of my ministry I dwelt chiefly upon the experiences of that period. I need not repeat what I said then. It was a season of severe discipline to us all, to the whole people of our country.

I will only say here, that so far from diverting my interest from the great subject of which I have been speaking, it harmonized with it and increased it. As I read the events and signs of that trying time, they became to me a living commentary upon the words of the Lord Jesus. Precepts of His, that had before seemed trite, began glowing and burning like revelations fresh from the Invisible. The parable of the Good Samaritan seemed to be made expressly for that hour. That scene in the synagogue at Nazareth, when all there were filled with wrath at what Jesus said,—how real was it, read by the light of the flames that consumed Pennsylvania Hall! As the truths of the New Testament, simple and divine, rose like suns and poured their light upon that long conflict, so did those days in return disclose a new and pointed significance in those simple pages, giving life to our Christian faith.

What a time, friends, has this been, the latter half of our first national century! It was a great day in history which gave the world the Printing-Press and the Protestant Reformation. But does not the last half century rival it? The railroad and the telegraph, mountains levelled, oceans and continents united, time and space vanishing, the huge sun made our submissive artist, the establishment of universal liberty over this broad land,—are not these things responding with literal obedience to the command of the ancient prophet: "Prepare ye the way of the Lord; make his path straight?"

It is a wonderful day, a great day of the Lord. We are stocks and stones if we do not catch the spirit, the generous spirit, of the Almighty breathing and brooding in countless unacknowledged ways over this mysterious human race. All things, like a host of prophets, are pointing us to an unimaginable destiny. The authority of the human soul over the visible Universe is becoming every hour more assured. We are not here to walk in a vain show, to live only for the lust of the eye, so soon to be quenched in dust, or for the pride which feeds on what withers almost at the touch. Our nature bears the ineradicable likeness of the Highest. The mystery of it is hidden in the mystery of all being, and the laws of our minds are revealed in the laws which hold the whole Creation together. We are not servants, we are sons, heirs of God; joint heirs with Jesus and all the good and great. And all is ours, ours to raise and enlarge our thoughts, to set us free from the corrupting bondage of the senses, to deepen our hunger and thirst for the only Living and the True, for the beauty of Holiness, the immortal life of God. And all our private experience; all our conflicts, our victories and our defeats; all the joys and sorrows which we have shared together,—the sacred memories that come to us to-day of parents, sons, daughters, and dear ones departed,—do they not throng around us now, and kindle our hearts with unutterable prayers for ourselves, for our children, and for one another?

NOTE

On the last anniversary of my ordination (the forty-ninth) I was led to dwell upon the Anti-slavery period of thirty years before the war of the rebellion. It was a period of intense interest, a great chapter in the history of our country.

There was one incident of those times to which I particularly referred a year ago, which I wish to record here, not on account of any great part that I had in it, but for the interesting character of the whole affair; and because, thinking it of some historical value, I am not aware that it has ever been recorded save in the daily press of the time. From a MS. record made some time ago of "Reminiscences," the following extract is transcribed:

"The most memorable occasion in my Anti-slavery experience was the annual meeting of the American Anti-slavery Society held in the 'Tabernacle,' as it was called, in New York, in May, 1850, I believe it was. I accepted an invitation to speak on that occasion, holding myself greatly honored thereby.

"Having no gift of extemporaneous speech, I prepared myself with the utmost pains. I went to New York the day before the meeting; saw Mr Garrison and Wendell Phillips. Mr Garrison said there would be a riot, as the Press had been doing its utmost to inflame the public mind against the Abolitionists.

"When the meeting was opened, the large hall, said to be the largest then in New York, capable of holding some thousands, was apparently full. The vast majority of the audience were doubtless friendly to the object of the meeting.

"Mr Garrison, Wendell Phillips, Edmund Quincy, Isaac Hopper, Francis Jackson, Frederick Douglass, and other faithful servants of the cause, were present on the platform.

"I saw friends here and there among the audience. I was surprised to recognize there a son of Judge Kane of this city (afterwards Col. T. Kane). I had some previous acquaintance with him, and knew him to be a young man of ardent temperament, open to generous ideas. I supposed then, and still suppose, that he was drawn there accidentally by curiosity. After a prayer by the Rev. Henry Grew, Mr Garrison made the opening speech, strong, bold, and characteristic.

"He had spoken only a few moments when he was interrupted by what sounded like a burst of applause; but as there was nothing special to call it forth, and as it proceeded from one little portion of the audience, I asked Wendell Phillips, who sat next to me, what it meant.

'It means,' he said, 'that there is to be a row.' The interruption was repeated again and again. A voice shouted some rude questions to Mr Garrison.

"Mr Garrison bore himself with the serenity of a summer's evening, answering: 'My friend, if you will wait till I get through, I will give you the information you ask for.' He succeeded in finishing his speech. I was to speak next. But the instant Mr Garrison ended, there came down upon the platform from the gallery which was connected with it, an individual, with a company of roughs at his back, who proved to be no less a person than the then well-known Isaiah Rynders. He began shouting and raving.

"I was not aware of being under any apprehension of personal violence. We were all like General Jackson's cotton-bales at New Orleans. Our demeanor made it impossible for the rioters to use any physical force against us. Young Kane, however, leaped upon the platform, and, pressing through to me, in a tone of great excitement, exclaimed: 'They shall not touch a hair of your head!' Mr Garrison said to Rynders in the quietest manner conceivable, 'You ought not to interrupt us. We go upon the principle of hearing everybody. If you wish to speak, I will keep order, and you shall be heard.' But Rynders was not in a state of mind to listen to reason. He had not come there for that, but to break up the meeting.

"The Hutchinsons, who were wont to sing at the Anti-slavery meetings, were in the gallery, and they attempted to raise a song, to soothe the savages with music. But it was of no avail. Rynders drowned their fine voices with noise and shouting. The chief of the police came upon the platform, and asked Mr Garrison whether he desired him to arrest and remove Rynders & Co. Mr Garrison answered: 'We desire nothing of you. We can take care of ourselves. You probably know your duty.' The

officer did nothing. In this scene of confusion, young
Kane became intensely excited. He rushed up to
Rynders, and shook his fist in his face. He said to me
with the deepest emphasis: 'If he touches Mr Garrison,
I'll *kill* him!' But Mr Garrison's composure was more
than a coat of mail. Rynders, indisposed to speak himself, brought forward a man to speak for him and his
party. Mr Francis Jackson and I were, the while, holding young Kane down in his seat to keep him from
breaking out into some act of violence. He was the most
dangerous element on our side. Rynders's substitute
professed a willingness that I should speak first (I was
down on the placards to follow Mr Garrison), provided
I did not make a long speech.

"Accordingly, I spoke my little, anxiously prepared
word. I never recall that hour without blessing myself
that I was called to speak precisely at that moment. At
any other stage of the proceedings, it would have been
wretchedly out of place.

"As it was, my speech fitted in almost as well as if it
had been impromptu, although a sharp eye might easily
have discovered that I was speaking *memoriter*. Rynders
interrupted me again and again, exclaiming that I lied,
that I was personal, but he ended with applauding me!
Rynders's man then came forward, rather dull and tire-
some in speech. It was his own friends who interrupted
him occasionally, Mr Garrison calling them to order.

"His argument was, that the blacks are not human
beings. Mr Garrison whispered to me while he was
speaking, that the speaker had formerly been a com-
positor in the office of the *Liberator*.

"He ended at last, and then Frederick Douglass was
loudly called for. Mr Douglass came forward, exqui-
sitely neat in his dress.

"'The gentleman who has just spoken,' he began, 'has

undertaken to prove that the blacks are not human beings. He has examined our whole conformation, from top to toe. I cannot follow him in his argument. I will assist him in it, however. I offer myself for your examination. Am I a man?' To this interrogatory instantly there came from the audience a thunderous affirmative. Rynders was standing right by the side of Mr Douglass, and when the response died away, he exclaimed in a hesitating way: 'But you're not a black man!' 'Then,' retorted Douglass, 'I'm your brother.' 'Ah,—ah,' said Rynders, hesitatingly, 'only half brother.' The effect upon the audience need not be described; it may readily be imagined. Mr Douglass then went on, complaining of Horace Greeley, who had recently said in his paper that the blacks did nothing for themselves. 'When I first came North,' said Mr Douglass, 'I went to the most decided Anti-slavery merchant in the North, and sought employment on a ship he was building, and he told me that if he were to give me work, every white operative would quit, and yet Mr Greeley finds fault with us that we do not help ourselves!' This criticism of Greeley pleased Rynders, who bore that gentleman no good will, and he added a word to Douglass's against Greeley. 'I am happy,' said Douglass, 'to have the assent of my half brother here,' pointing to Rynders, and convulsing the audience with laughter. After this, Rynders, finding how he was played with, took care to hold his peace; but some one of Rynders's company in the gallery undertook to interrupt the speaker. 'It's of no use,' said Mr Douglass; '*I've Captain Rynders here to back me.*' 'We were born here,' he went on to say, 'we have made the clothes that you wear, and the sugar that you put into your tea, and we mean to stay here and do all we can for you.' 'Yes!' cried a voice from the gallery, 'and you'll cut our throats!' 'No,' said the speaker, '*we'll only cut your hair.*' When the laughter ceased, Mr Douglass proceeded to say: 'We mean to stay here, and do all we can for every one, be he a man, or be he a monkey,' accompanying these last words with a wave of his hand towards the quarter whence the interruption had come. He concluded with saying that he saw his friend, Samuel Ward, present, and he would ask him to step forward. All eyes were instantly turned to the back of the platform, or stage rather, so dramatic was the scene, and there, amidst a group, stood a large man, so black that, as Wendell Phillips said, when he shut his eyes, you could not see him. Had I observed him before, I should have wondered what brought him there, accounting him as fresh from Africa. He belonged to the political wing of the Abolition party (Gerritt Smith's), and had wandered into the meeting, never expecting to be called upon to speak. At the call of Frederick Douglass, he came to the front, and, as he approached, Rynders exclaimed: 'Well, this is the original nigger!' 'I've heard of the magnanimity of Captain Rynders,' said Ward, 'but the half has not been told me!' And then he went on with a noble voice, and his speech was such a strain of eloquence as I never heard excelled before or since.

"'There are more than fifty people here,' said he, 'who may remember me as a little black boy running about the streets of New York. I have always been called nigger, and the only consolation that has been offered me for being called nigger was, that, when I die and go to heaven, I shall be white. If'—and here, with an earnestness of tone and manner that thrilled one to the very marrow, he continued—'If I cannot go to heaven as black as God made me, let me go down to hell, and dwell with the devils forever!'

"The effect was beyond description.

"'This gentleman,' he said, 'who denies our humanity,

has examined us scientifically, but I know something of
anatomy. I have kept school, and I have had pupils,
from the jet black up to the soft dissolving views, and
I've seen white boys with retreating foreheads and pro-
jecting jaws, and, as Dickens says, in Nicholas Nickleby,
of Smike, you might knock here all day,' tapping his
forehead, 'and find nobody at home.' In this strain, he
went on, ruling the large audience with Napoleonic power.
Coal-black as he was, he was an emperor, *pro tempore*.

"When he ceased speaking, the time had expired for
which the Tabernacle was engaged, and we had to ad-
journ. Never was there a grander triumph of intelli-
gence, of mind, over brute force. Two colored men, whose
claim to be considered human was denied, had, by mere
force of intellect, overwhelmed their maligners with confusion. As the audience was thinning out, I went down
on the floor to see some friends there. Rynders came
by. I could not help saying to him, 'How shall we
thank you for what you have done for us to-day?' 'Well,'
said he, 'I do not like to hear my country abused, but
that last thing that you said, that's the truth.' That last
thing was, I believe, a simple assertion of the right of the
people to think and speak freely.

"Judging by his physiognomy and his scriptural name
Isaiah, I took Captain Rynders to be of Yankee descent.
Notwithstanding his violent behavior, he yet seemed to
be a man accessible to the force of truth. I found that
Lucretia Mott had the same impressions of him. She
saw him a day or two afterwards in a restaurant on
Broadway, and she sat down at his table, and entered
into conversation with him. As he passed out of the
restaurant, he asked Mr McKim, who was standing there,
waiting for Mrs Mott, whether Mrs Mott were his mother.
Mr McKim replied in the negative. 'She's a good sen-
sible woman,' said Rynders.

"Never before or since have I been so deeply moved as on that occasion. Depths were stirred in me never before reached. For days afterwards, when I undertook to tell the story, my head instantly began to ache. Mr Garrison said, if the papers would only faithfully report the scene, it would revolutionize public sentiment. As it was, they heaped all sorts of ridicule upon us. I cheerfully accepted my share, entirely willing to pass for a fool in the eyes of the world. It was a cheap price to pay for the privilege of witnessing such a triumph. I was taken quite out of myself. I came home, stepping like Malvolio. I had shared in the smile of Freedom, the belle and beauty of the world.

"A day or two after my return home, I met one of my parishioners in the street, and stopped and told him all about my New York visit. He listened to me with a forced smile, and told me that there had been some thought of calling an indignation meeting of the church to express the mortification felt at my going and mixing myself up with such people. I had hardly given a thought to the effect at home, so full was I of the interest and glory of the occasion. I ought to have preached on the Sunday following from the words: '*He has gone to be a guest with a man who is a sinner!*'"

MEETING

OF THE

First Congregational Society of Unitarian Christians,

IN PHILADELPHIA,

HELD IN THE CHURCH, TENTH AND LOCUST STREETS,

JANUARY 12, 1875,

IN COMMEMORATION OF THE

FIFTIETH ANNIVERSARY

OF

Rev. W. H. FURNESS, D.D.,

AS PASTOR OF THEIR CHURCH.

On the evening of January 12th, 1875, the meeting of the First Unitarian Society, in commemoration of the fiftieth anniversary of the pastorate of the Rev. Dr. Furness, was held in the church.

The following ministers were present:

Rev. Dr. John H. Morison,
Rev. Dr. S. K. Lothrop,
Rev Dr. James Freeman Clarke,
Rev. Dr. James T. Thompson,
Rev. Dr. C. A. Bartol,
Rev. Dr. H. W. Bellows,
Rev. Dr. A. P. Putnam,
Rev. F. Israel,
Rev. R. R. Shippen,
Rev. Wm. O. White,
Rev. J. F. W. Ware,
Rev. Wm. C. Gannett,
Rev. E. H. Hall,
Rev. J. W. Chadwick,
Rev. Thos. J. Mumford,
Rev. C. G. Ames.

The church was profusely but tastefully hung with festoons of evergreen; on the wall, behind the pulpit, was a large cross; among the festoons which overhung it were the figures "1825" and "1875" in white and green flowers; while in front of the pulpit, covering the communion table and all the approaches to it, were growing tropical plants, amid which was a profusion of vases, baskets, and bouquets of natural flowers, with smilax distributed here and there in delicate fringes or festoons.

The regular quartette choir of the church, consisting of

Mrs. W. D. Dutton,	Soprano,
Mrs. Isaac Ashmead, Jr.,	Contralto,
Mr. E. Dillingham,	Tenor,
Mr. F. G. Cauffman,	Bass,

was on this occasion assisted by

Miss Cassidy,	Miss Jennie Cassidy,
Miss Cooper,	Mrs. Roberts,
Mr. A. H. Rosewig,	Mr. W. W. Gilchrist,

under the direction of Mr. W. D. Dutton, organist of the church.

PROCEEDINGS.

At half-past seven o'clock the exercises of the evening commenced, as follows:

Music.

Tenor solo and chorus, ... MENDELSSOHN.
"Oh, come, let us worship," from 95th Psalm.

Mr. Henry Winsor, Chairman of the Committee of Arrangements, in opening the meeting made the following remarks:

The occasion of our meeting here this evening is so well known to all present that there is no need of any formal announcement of it. We thought some time ago that this anniversary of our pastor's ordination, when the half century of his ministration here is complete, ought to be in some way marked and commemorated; and as one of the things for that purpose,—as the best means perhaps to that end, we invited friends in New England and elsewhere to be with us here to-night; and I am glad to say that some of them have come; as many perhaps as we had reason to expect at this inclement season.

And now, speaking for this Society, I want to say to them that their presence is a special joy to us; a greater joy than it could be on a similar occasion to any society in New England; for there Unitarians are at home, and each society has many neighbors with whom it can commune, and to whom it can look for sympathy, and, if need be, for assistance. But this Society of Unitarian Christians has long been alone in this great city, having no connection with any religious society here and communing with none. And so, as I said, your presence on this occasion is a real joy to us, and, on behalf of the Society, I heartily thank you for it. But we are here— we of the congregation are here—not to speak but to listen; and I will now ask Dr. Morison, of Massachusetts, to pray for us.

Prayer by Rev. Dr. John H. Morison.

Almighty and most merciful Father, we beseech Thee to open our hearts to all the gracious and hallowed associations of this hour. Help us so to enter into the spirit of this hour, that all holy influences may be around us, that our hearts may be touched anew, that we may be brought together more tenderly, and lifted up, with a deeper gratitude and reverence, to Thee, the Fountain of all good, the Giver of every good and perfect gift. We thank Thee, most merciful Father, for the ministry which has been modestly carrying on its beneficent work here through these fifty years. We thank Thee for all the lives which have been helped by it to see and to do Thy will, and which have been made more beautiful and holy by being brought into quicker sympathies with whatever is beautiful in the world without, and whatever is lovely in the world within. We thank Thee for the inspiring words which have been here spoken, brought home to the consciences of this congregation by the life which stood behind them, to make men more earnest to search after what is true and to do what is right. We thank Thee, our Father in heaven, for all the sweet and tender and far-reaching hopes, too vast for this world, which have been opening here, begun upon the earth and fulfilled in other worlds, in more immediate union with the spirits of the just made perfect; and we thank Thee for all the solemn memories here, through which the dear and honored forms of those to whom we who are aged now looked up once as to our fathers and teachers rise again transfigured and alive before us. We thank Thee for all those who have been with us in the ministry of Christ, and under the ministry of Christ, gracious souls, rejoicing with us in the work which they and we have been permitted to do, and now, as our trust is, numbered among Thy saints in glory everlasting. And while we here render thanks to Thee for the ministry so long and so faithfully fulfilled in this place, so allying itself to all that is sweet in our human affections, to all that is beautiful in the world of nature and of art, to all that is holy in the domestic relations, to all that is strong and true in the defence of human rights, to the deepest human interests and to thy love, uniting in grateful reverence for the past, we would also ask Thy holy Spirit to dwell with Thy servant, to inspire him still with thoughts which shall keep his soul always young, his spirit always fresh, for long years yet to come, with increasing ripeness and increasing devotedness; and that he may long continue to walk in and out here amid the silent benedictions of those who have learned to love and honor him.

Our Father in heaven, help us that whatever may be said at this time may be in harmony with the occasion. While we here rise up in prayer and thanksgiving to Thee, grant that Thy heavenly benediction may rest on pastor and people, that Thy loving spirit may turn our human wishes into heavenly blessings, and that the words and example of Him who came into the world, not to do his own will but the will of Him that sent him, may comfort and strengthen us; and that the life which has been such an inspiration and joy and quickening power to our friend may be to all of us still an incentive to holiness, and an inspiration to all pure and heavenly thoughts.

And now, most merciful Father, grant to us all, that it may be good for us to be here—so gracious and so hallowed is the time—and Thine, through Jesus Christ our Lord, be the kingdom and the power and the glory forever and ever. Amen.

Music.

Soprano solo and chorus, ... Spohr.
"How lovely are thy dwellings fair!"

Mr. Winsor then spoke as follows:

At the ordination of Dr. Furness, fifty years ago, the sermon was delivered by one eminent among Unitarian Christians, by whom his memory will be long cherished and honored, Henry Ware, Jr., and for this reason I ask to speak first of all here to-night his son, Rev. John F. W. Ware, of Boston, Mass.

ADDRESS OF REV. JOHN F. W. WARE.

FRIENDS OF THIS CHRISTIAN SOCIETY: I have no other claim to be standing here to-night and participating in your service than the one just mentioned—that I am the son of the man who, fifty years ago this day, preached the sermon at the ordination of his friend, William

Henry Furness, and what may seem to you my fitness is indeed my unfitness. Proud as I am in being the son of a man so much honored, loved, and remembered, I never feel it quite right in any way to try to represent him, and had I known that this was to be a part of the consequences of my journey I think I should have stayed at home.

But during the hours that I have been on the way my thoughts have been busy with that fifty years ago, thinking of the goodly company who, "in the winter wild," came down here from New England that they might plant this vine in the vineyard of the Lord. And none of them who came at that time to plant are permitted to be here to-night to help us gather the rich and ripened clusters. It showed, I think, the love that these men had for, and the confidence that they had in, their young friend, that they should have come, in that inclement time, this long journey by stage, taking them days and nights of discomfort as it did. I think that there was no sweeter household word in that dear old home of mine than "Brother Furness"—the old-fashioned way in which ministers used to talk of one another, which we of to-day have forgotten. In those times it meant something; to-day we don't feel as if it did, so we have dropped it. I think there was no name so sweet outside of the closest family ties as that name, and we children grew—my sister and myself—to have always the deepest love for the man that our father loved; and as time went by, and young manhood came, I looked forward to the hearing of the tones of that voice, and the seeing of that smile, and the touching of that hand, as among the bright and pleasant things—a sort of condescending, it always seemed to me to be, of one who was in a sphere higher up than I ever hoped to climb to. Then, as I grew older, I remember the audacity with which I offered him "a labor of love" in this church, and I remember I trembled after I had done it; and I remember how he thanked me, and how he criticized me, and the criticizing was a great deal better than the thanking. It was very deep; it meant a good deal, and it has not been forgotten.

Fortunate man! he who came into this city fifty years ago; fortunate in the place, and the time of his birth; fortunate in the education he had had and the faith he had imbibed; fortunate in the place he had gone to, not to be coddled among friends, emasculated by being surrounded by those who thought just as he did, but thrown out by God's will into this outpost, where he could grow, as we cannot where we are surrounded by those of our own preference and method of thinking; fortunate in the bent of his study, in the opportunity to unfold the beautiful life of Jesus; fortunate in being of those who stood up for the slave; fortunate in having lived to see the issue of the work that his heart was engaged in; fortunate in being now crowned by the love and benediction of his people, and retiring calmly and sweetly from the work of life, still to dwell among those who have loved him these years long. Oh, fortunate man! God bless him, and continue him here many years yet, your joy, your companion, your guide, and your friend.

Not many of us shall see our fiftieth anniversary, for more and more this profession of ours becomes a thing of yesterday, to-day, and to-morrow alone. Very few occasions there will be again to meet together to celebrate the fiftieth anniversary of a minister's settlement.

Let us treasure the memory of this occasion. Let it go with us who are here to our homes and our works, and may it remain here with you a thought and memory and a help; and as, in the beginning, this church drew its life and its first impulse through a little band of sturdy and steady and upright laymen, so in the time that lies before you, lay friends of this Society, remember that it is not the past upon which you can lean—the work that has been done by the servant who retires. It is the future in which you are to hope, and the character of that future must be largely your work. With this simple word, knowing that there are many gentlemen here who are to speak, and will speak more wisely and properly than I, I ask Mr. Gannett to follow me.

Rev. Dr. Furness then came forward, and said :

MY DEAR FRIENDS: I am very doubtful about the propriety of my being present on this occasion, not because any deserts of mine would call forth any extravagant eulogium, but because I know the kind hearts of my friends. They would say things which would make me very uncomfortable. But just before I came from home I got a letter from our friend, Mr. Weld, minister of the church in Baltimore. He has sent us from the church in Baltimore two communion cups—silver cups—as a token of kind fellowship and recognition of this anniversary from the church in Baltimore. They wished to have an inscription placed on them, but they had no time; indicating that they were gifts from the church in Baltimore. So I thought I would bring them down without delay, and put them upon the table, if there was any room for them.

In all the kind words which my brethren say about me, I think there is a good deal put in. Just like the old man who took notes of his minister's sermons, and when he read them over to the minister, the minister said, "Stop! stop! I did not say that." "I know you didn't," he said; "but I put it in to make sense of it." So, I think, on this occasion, there will be a good deal put in. If you will allow me, I will go and sit down at the other end of the room, and if they get a little too strong I can run out. I was entreated to come here and show myself. I am very grateful to you for your kind attention.

Address of William C. Gannett.

Like Mr. Ware, I only speak as the son of the right man. The right man stood by Dr. Furness' side fifty years ago, and gave him the right hand of fellowship. I know not whether there are any here that saw the sight or heard the words; perhaps of all he only. The air seems full, to me, at least, of the memories of the other one. And to you who sit and listen, the air must seem full of the very spirit of communion that these cups just given symbolize. There ought to have been a white head here; there ought to have been dark eyes; there ought to have been a ringing voice; there ought to have been a voice that would have been full of tenderness as he stood at this side of the fifty years,—as he then stood at the other side,—and said the words of an old man's fellowship. He would to-day, as then, have been just six months Dr. Furness' senior in the work. I suppose one can imagine anybody, any old person, as young, easier than he can his own father or his own mother. I cannot conceive the one whom I call father standing here, or in the place which this church represents, as a young man of twenty-four speaking to a young man of twenty-three, and bidding him welcome into the work which he called partaking in the work of heaven; bidding him welcome into its pleasures; bidding him welcome into its pains,—for he had been six months a minister, and in those first six months of a minister's life he knows a great deal of the pains that accompany it. It so happened that just after I got your kind invitation to come, I happened to lay my hand upon the manuscript of that right hand of fellowship, and not having time to read it then, I brought it with me in the cars; and only three or four hours ago I was reading the very words, and reading from the very paper which, fifty years ago, was held and read from, and to which Dr. Furness listened. It does seem to me as if the reader were here now to say, "God bless you, old friend, for having stood ever faithful to the end." I almost think he *is* saying it; and if he is, I know it comes with just that feeling: "God bless you, old friend, for having stood faithful to the end; for having fulfilled all and more than all the words that then I said to you." And that is all I have to say. I was asked to pass the word along to another boy of the old men. Your father and my father and Dr. Hall were classmates. Will Edward Hall speak for his father?

Address of Rev. Edward H. Hall, of Worcester, Mass.

I hardly know to what I owe this pleasure, for it is a great one to me, of joining my thoughts with others tonight, at so early a point of our gathering. I believe my claim is a double one, and I am willing and anxious to make it as large as possible, both as the successor of one who, fifty years ago, was present to give the charge to the people, and, still tenderer to me, the claim which has just been presented by the friend who preceded me. In that class, which I suppose stands eminent among the graduating classes of Cambridge for the number of men it has sent into our ministry, to say nothing of their quality, were the three whose names have just been

brought together, who had no greater pride, I believe,
than to have their names in common. And it is for me
one of the pleasantest memories which this hour brings
that they were not only classmates—my father and our
father to-night—but that for so long a time, through their
college course, they were in closest intimacy as room-
mates. And yet I should be sorry to think that this was
my only connection with this occasion. It was said, I
remember, of one of the finest and noblest of our officers
killed in the war, that of the many who had met him,
each one seemed to feel that he had made a special discovery of that man's noble character and fine traits, so
did the discovery overpower him, and so sure was he that
to no one else had it come as it did to him; and I am in-
clined to think that there is no one of these ministers
here to-night who does not feel as if his connection with
him whom we meet to-night to honor was something
special, as if the inspiration which he had drawn from
that source was one which no one but himself had got.
No qualification for our profession, I suppose, is higher
than the power of historic intuition; the power of seeing
things as they were; of reading the words and seeing behind them; the power that reproduces the past. Our
great historians are those who read the past in that way;
our great theologians are those who read the past as if
it were present, and feel a personal intercourse with those
who walked and spoke in those early days. They are
the holy men and apostles of to-day; they will always
be the apostles to the end of time, and I am glad to feel
that out of our numbers has come one whose power of
divining the past has shown itself so fine and true.

I can hardly help speaking about another feeling.
I am impressed to-night by the difference, the vast difference, between our fathers of a generation ago and
us who are upon the stage to-day. We look back rev-

erently to them; perhaps children always do to their fathers. It is barely possible that our children may look upon us in the same way. We look upon them as a group of men set apart by themselves—a kind of priesthood, conscious of the sanctity of their work. A sort of moral halo encircles their heads as we think of them, and we group them in just that affectionate way to which our friend before me has alluded, as a band of brothers. Will this generation of ministers ever look to their successors as they appear to us? I cannot believe it. That will not be our claim upon their honor or their regard. Happy for us if we can have any claim upon it; if men shall see that the second generation of ministers took bravely up the work that was half done, uttered the words that were still unspoken, continued in the path which the fathers cannot longer tread, and proved that it takes more than one generation to do the work which Unitarianism is born to accomplish.

But I have no more claim upon your time, and close by introducing to you, as I have been asked, the Rev. Dr. Lothrop, of Boston.

Rev. Dr. S. K. Lothrop spoke as follows:

MY CHRISTIAN FRIENDS: I have but a few words to say, and I rise to say these simply that I may more fully express what my presence here implies, my deep sympathy and interest in this occasion.

There are scenes and events in life which, from their simplicity and beauty, and the moral grandeur which always mingles more or less with everything simple and beautiful, can gain nothing from human lips. Eloquence can coin no words that shall impress them upon the heart and conscience more deeply than they impress themselves. This occasion is one of these events. We meet here to-night—this company, the members of this church, these brethren from distant and different parts of the country —to commemorate fifty years of faithful and devoted service in the Christian ministry, and rhetoric can add nothing to the moral dignity and grandeur of this fact, that is not contained in the simplest statement or expression of it. We meet to do honor and reverence to one, who, from the earliest aspirations of his youth to the later aspirations and ever enlarging service of his manhood, has known no object but truth, no law but duty, no master but conscience, and who, under the inspiration and guidance of these has wrought a noble work in this city, made full proof of his ministry, and given a glorious illustration of the power of that faith, " which is the victory that overcometh the world."

The Unitarian Congregationalists recognize a large personal freedom and individuality. Among the brethren present and all called by our name who are absent, there are wide differences of theological thought and opinion; and some of us may not entirely concur in all the conclusions—the result of Christian thought and study— which our honored brother, the pastor of this church, in his fifty years of noble service, may have presented in this pulpit or given to the public through the press. But however he may differ from him on some points, no one who has read what he has published, can fail to perceive or refuse to acknowledge the spirit of devout reverence, love, faith, the large and glorious humanity that everywhere breathe in his words; while every one familiar with his long life-work in this city, every one who has known him intimately, had opportunity to study and observe his character, to mark its mingled firmness and gentleness, sweetness and strength, its martyr spirit adhering to conscientious convictions and carrying them out at whatever cost or sacrifice, its loyal spirit, faithful to Christ and truth according to honest and sincere conviction, every one who knows and has witnessed how these things have pervaded and animated his life, character, work, cannot fail to cherish toward him a sentiment of reverence and honor; and amid all differences of opinion there may be between us, I yield to no one in the strength and sincerity with which I cherish this sentiment in my own heart. When I visited him at his house to-day, I could not but feel that while years had not abated one jot of the vigor of his intellect or the warmth of his heart, they had added largely to that something, I know not what to call it, that indescribable charm, which has given him a place in every heart that has ever known him, and made us his brethren (I am only uttering what they will all acknowledge) always disposed to sit at his feet in love and admiration.

I am one of the oldest, probably the oldest of our ministers present. Dr. Furness' ordination antedates mine, which occurred in February, 1829, only by four years and a month. As regards term of service my name is close to his on our list of living clergymen, and I remember, as if it were but yesterday, his ordination fifty years ago to-day, and can distinctly recall the deep interest with which it was spoken of that evening in the family circle of the late Dr. Kirkland at Cambridge, of which I was then a member. I had but slight personal acquaintance with Dr. Furness, however, till thirteen years after this, in 1838, when suffering from ill health he was unable for several months to discharge his duties. His pulpit was supplied by clergymen from Boston and the neighborhood, and as he had many loving friends and warm admirers in Brattle Square Society, they were very willing to release me for six weeks, that I might come to Philadelphia and preach for him. This visit and service brought me into more intimate acquaintance with him and this Society. The pleasant memories of that period, fresh in my heart to this day, were prominent among the manifold recollections that prompted, nay, constrained me to come and unite my sympathies with yours on this occasion. It is a glad occasion, yet there is something solemn and sad about it. Like all anniversaries, it has a double meaning, makes a double appeal to us. It gives a tongue to memory, calls up the shadows of the past, brings before us the forms of those we have loved and lost; we see their smiles; we hear their voices; and as I stand here to-night, and look back upon those fifty years, and call to mind the venerable fathers of our faith, whom I knew and loved and honored in the early days of my professional life, Drs. Bancroft, Ripley, Thayer, Harris, Pierce, Nichols of Portland, Parker of Portsmouth, Flint of Salem, and bring before me the Boston Association when it numbered among its members Channing, Lowell, Parkman, Ware, Greenwood, Frothingham, Pierpont, Young, and last, though not least, that great apostle who has just departed, Dr. Walker, I feel as if I had lived a century, and was a very old man. I feel, however, that life is not to be measured by years, and I hope, mean always to try to keep as young, bright, joyous, and buoyant as Dr. Furness seemed this morning when I greeted him in his own house.

I sympathize in all that has been said here this evening, especially in all that has been said in relation to the future of this Society and its honored and beloved pastor. It is no longer a secret, I believe, that he intends to ask a release from further service. I am sure, my friends, that all the brethren present will leave with you their loving benediction, and the hope that something of his mantle may fall upon whoever comes to try to fill his place. The whole of that mantle, in all its beauty, grandeur, and simplicity, you cannot expect any man to have or wear; if you find a successor wearing a goodly portion of it you will have great reason to rejoice, to thank God and be of good courage. As for Dr. Furness himself, we leave with him our gratitude and reverence, and our devout wish that the sweetest serenity and peace and moral glory may mark his remaining years; and for ourselves, who have come from far and near to hold this jubilee with him, we all hope to gather here to-night and carry away with us on the morrow memories, inspirations, influences that shall quicken us to fresh zeal and effort in our several spheres of work, determined to be faithful and persevere unto the end, whether that end cover twenty, thirty or forty, or, as may be the case with some of us, fifty years of professional service.

Rev. Dr. James Freeman Clarke, of Boston, being called upon to read a poem written for the occasion, spoke as follows:

A great many years ago I was journeying from Kentucky to Boston, and passing through Philadelphia, I could not deny myself the pleasure of going to see our dear friend, Mr. Furness, and he was then full of the thoughts which were afterward published in his first book, concerning Jesus of Nazareth. I spent the whole morning talking with him, and when the morning was through, said he, "Stay a little longer;" and I said, "I will wait till night before I go;" and I spent the afternoon talking with him, and when the night came, he had not finished speaking, and I had not finished listening. So I spent another day. We talked in the morning, we talked in the afternoon, and we talked in the evening. I still had not heard all I wanted to, and so I stayed the third day, and, of course, Brother Furness is very much associated in my mind with his studies on this subject, which has led me to take the tone which you will find in these lines :

    Where is the man to comprehend the Master,
      The living human Jesus—He who came
    To follow truth through triumph or disaster,
      And glorify the gallows and its shame?

    No passive Christ, yielding and soft as water ;
      Sweet, but not strong; with languid lip and eye ;
    A patient lamb, led silent to the slaughter ;
      A monkish Saviour, only sent to die.

    Nor that result of Metaphysic Ages;
      Christ claiming to be God, yet man indeed—
    Christ dried to dust in theologic pages ;
      Our human brother frozen in a creed !

    But that all-loving one, whose heart befriended
      The humblest sufferer under God's great throne ;
    While, in his life, humanity ascended
      To loftier heights than earth had ever known.

    All whose great gifts were natural and human ;
      Loving and helping all; the great, the mean ;
    The friend of rich and poor, of man and woman ;
      And calling no one common or unclean.

    Most lofty truth in household stories telling,
      Which to the souls of wise and simple go ;
    Forever in the Father's bosom dwelling—
      Forever one with human hearts below.

    Not in the cloister, or professor's study
      God sets the teacher for this work apart,—
    But where the life-drops, vigorous and ruddy,
      Flow from the heart to hand, from hand to heart.

He only rightly understands *this* Saviour,
  Who walks himself the same highway of truth ;
Unfolding, with like frank and bold behavior,
  Such earnest manhood from such spotless youth.

Whose widening sympathy avoids extremes,
  Who loves all lovely things, afar, anear—
Who still respects in age his youthful dreams,
  Untouched by skeptic-doubt or cynic-sneer.

Who, growing older, yet grows young again,
  Keeping his youth of heart;—whose spirit brave
Follows with Jesus, breaking every chain,
  And bringing liberty to every slave.

To him, to-night, who, during fifty years,
  For truths unrecognized has dared the strife,
In spite of fashion's law or wisdom's fears,
  We come to thank him for a noble life.

He needs no thanks, but will accept that love,
  The grateful love, inevitably given
To those who waken faith in things above,
  And mingle with our days a light from heaven.

And most of all, who shows us how to find
  The Great Physician for all earthly ill—
The true Reformer, calm and bold and kind,
  Who came not to destroy but to fulfil.

And thus this church grows into holy ground
  So full of Jesus that our souls infer
That we, like Bunyan's Pilgrim, must have found
  At last " The House of the Interpreter."

Dr. Clarke called upon Rev. Dr. Bartol to speak, who said :

MY FRIENDS: I certainly ought in all sincerity, and I certainly do in all humility, thank the committee for in-

viting one, so devoid of all conventional virtue, with no
place in any conference, standing for the desert—yet not
quite, I think, belonging to the tribe of Ishmael, for my
hand is against no man, and no man's hand, I think, is
against me,—to say even one word. But let me tell you
there is good ecclesiastical blood in the family. I throw
myself on one who is worthy, I am sure, and popular in
this church, a cousin by blood. I think there is a good
deal of vicarious atonement in him; and I hope his
righteousness will be imputed to me, though I do not
mean to make him a scapegoat for my sins.

Notwithstanding what my brother has said, I shall call
him not only *brother* but *John Ware;* and because of what
he said we shall all be convinced that this is a real
brotherhood in spirit as in name after all. I call it a
very goodly fellowship, not only of the prophets but of
the people to-night. And that is the thought that comes
into my mind in regard to it. Here our brother and
father Furness, your minister, has brought all these
brethren together who stand in thought so wide apart.
Is it not a real fellowship? I need not mention the
names to show you how wide a space of thought they
measure, and the beauty and power of a man's fellowship. It is not to be determined by the number of his
disciples or followers, by the largeness of the congregation he can gather, or the crowds that hang on his lips;
but by the measure which all those men, be they more or
fewer, make in the world of ideas, which is also the world
of love; for a man's parallax, that twenty friends may
make for him, is a larger parallax than a million friends
may make. And I think it is, in spite of our dear friend's
utter modesty, an occasion of joy with him. It should
be an occasion of joy that he reaches so far out on either
hand, and gathers such a company together. It is a real
fellowship, a real brotherhood, a real fatherhood; and while

these young men have been speaking—and we have not
begun with the eldest, even to the last, but have begun
the other way—it seemed to me as if the almond blossoms
from the old heads which we remember, as well as see,
have been dropping upon some of our heads, and that
they have shed them upon us. We are glad for that fellowship. It is rich beyond measure.

I had a letter from our dear Brother Dewey. He says
in this letter, speaking of the death of Dr. Walker, "He
seems to say to me, 'Your turn next.'" Ah, "*sad!*" Did
I hear that word? No, not sad. Death is not sad;
departure is not sad; ascending is not sad. Death is
nothing. But what is meant by our thought? I said to
my dear friend, Dr. Bellows, last night as we were talking,
"How strange it would be, when we came each one of us
to die, to find that death, which we have thought so much
of, is nothing to think of! Death at last and for the
first time takes everlasting leave of us. Death will just
so surely depart from us as we come to die. And in the
article of dying it will depart."

It is well that I should close with this single thought
of fellowship. Providence has been working very wonderfully and very mightily, with all these great causes
which have had great sway in the modern world, through
this gospel of free thought. I call it a gospel,—a gospel
of humanity, this loving gospel to bring people together.
I do not like the word *fellowship* as an active verb. I
never could speak of *fellowshipping* one. Fellowship is
the result of being true to our own conviction one to
another; coming and sitting in the circle that takes in
the heaven as well as the earth,—and I will finish my
little talk with what perhaps is as yet an unedited fact
or story, of one of those other elders, not so very old, who
have gone to the majority. Samuel Joseph May illustrated this bond of fellowship; how God will have it, that

we must be brethren and fellows, whether we will or not. He told me that one day, a great many years ago, it must now be between thirty or forty years, he was returning from an anti-slavery meeting, on a steamer, when a theological conversation arose between some parties, and one man was pleased to denounce Unitarians very severely; and perhaps some of you remember what that denunciation was of the Unitarian Doctrine. It was infidel, it was atheistic, it was all that was bad. Mr. May listened quietly until the man got through, who had the sympathy of others, and then frankly, like himself, said, "I must tell you, sir, that I am myself one of those dreadful Unitarians." "Indeed, indeed," said the man. "I have listened to you with great pleasure at the anti-slavery meeting; would you allow me to have a little conversation with you at the other end of the boat, privately?" "With the utmost pleasure," said Mr. May. They took their departure from the little circle to the bow of the boat. As the man was about to open his converting speech, Mr. May said: "Now before we proceed to our little controversy, I wish to ask you one question. Do you believe it is possible in this matter of theology, I after all may be right and you may be wrong?" "No, I don't believe it is possible," said the man. "Then, then," said Mr. May, "I think there is no advantage in our having any further conversation." Mr. May had his place nevertheless in that man's heart: for we do not choose our fellows. God chooses our fellows for us. A man said one day: "I heard that transcendental lecturer speak. He got his thought into my mind, and the worst of it is, I can't get it out." Be true to your conviction; for that is the charm, the beauty, the holiness! And then—I must say it, yes, I must say it in spite of Dr. Furness' presence—not your *thought* alone, but *you* will get into the heart of every man or woman who has the slightest knowledge of you. And the man and the woman will love you, and the time will come when they will not want to get you out of their mind.

Rev. Dr. Thompson, of Jamaica Plain, Mass., then addressed the meeting as follows:

MY FRIENDS: I feel a good deal of embarrassment in taking my place on the platform, having received no hint that any word would be expected of me.

If I were as old and gray as some of the brethren who have preceded me, I might perhaps follow in their severely sober strain, but you will have to take me as I am. Before touching on what more immediately concerns the occasion, let me frankly confess to having brought with me a slight pique against the venerated pastor of this church, and you shall know how it happened. About ten years ago—it will be ten in April—the Sunday after the first National Conference in New York, I was seated in this church. Three or four of us ministers had come on to attend the worship; by what attraction you can well imagine. Robert Collyer preached the sermon, one of the best he ever preached, that on "Hurting and Healing Shadows." Now you all know Dr. Furness' great fondness for conferences and such like, only he never goes to them! Well, I think he must have been a little uneasy while Collyer was preaching from having heard of the great enthusiasm which prevailed in the recent conference, and from regretting, though he did not say so, that circumstances, or something, had prevented his being there to share it. While he sat in the pulpit under this "hurting shadow" he was thinking very likely—but I do not assert it as a fact—how he could extemporize something here that would bear a resemblance to what we had been doing and enjoying in New York; and he hit on a plan. So, immediately after Brother

Collyer had finished, our excellent friend arose, looking exactly as he does to-night, and, with that peculiar twinkle under his spectacles and expression about the mouth which none of you will ever forget, said, that it had occurred to him that, as a number of ministers were present who had attended the New York conference, it might be interesting to the congregation to hear an account of it from their lips; and without further ceremony he would call upon them. When it came my turn he introduced me in this fashion; (and here comes in the pique of which I am going to free my mind). "This gentleman," said he (giving my name), "some of the *older* members of the society may perhaps remember to have heard preach here, I will not undertake to say precisely when, but it was some time within the present century!" Do you wonder that I have had a feeling about this insinuation? It was true that I had preached for him while yet a young man, and he about as old to my appreciation as he is now. It is also true that in the abundance of his kindness he wanted to say a pleasant thing about the sermon; and he did say it. And what do you think it was? I hope it is not too flattering for me to repeat after having carried it so long in my memory. He said: "Thompson, there was one capital word in your sermon, a capital word." "What was it?" I asked, surprised. "It was the word *intenerated;* where did you get it?" "From the dictionary," I meekly replied; "and you will find it there." And now I wish to say that if at any time within the last forty years you have heard that word "intenerated" from the lips of your minister you may know where it came from.

Dr. Furness: I have never used it once. (Laughter.)

What delightful reminiscences of my connection with this church!

And now let me come to the matter of the jubilee.

It happened to me less than a week ago to walk into the *sanctum* of our Brother Mumford, the accomplished editor of the Christian Register. I entered expecting to see my welcome in the generous smile with which he usually meets his friends. But instead of this, his face wore a most solemn expression, and he seemed to find it hard even to look at me. "What now?" thought I; "what have I been doing?" After a minute or two of suspense, I was relieved by his lifting his eyes pleasantly and saying: "I am doing up Dr. Furness," or words to that effect. I instantly remonstrated, saying it would spoil every man's speech who goes to Philadelphia, for they are all doing just what you are. They are all searching the volumes of the Christian Register and Christian Examiner, and other newspapers and periodicals to find out all they can in relation to the man and the ordination fifty years ago. But he was inflexible, saying that "he didn't mean that the Christian Register should be behind any of them." So he went on, and the result was the excellent notice of our friend which appeared last Saturday.

However, he did not give quite all the facts that link themselves in my mind with the ordination of Dr. Furness. It was a very remarkable year of ordinations in our Unitarian body, remarkable as to the number of them, and as to the character and future eminence of the men ordained, and the reputation of the ministers who ordained them. Let me refer to a few of them. Six months before the ordination here, June 30th, 1824, our beloved Brother Gannett had been ordained as the colleague of Dr. Channing; and, on the same day, his lifelong friend in the closest intimacy, the Rev. Calvin Lincoln, was ordained at Fitchburg. Then came this ordination; and in just a week after, January 19th, followed that of the Rev. Alexander Young, over the New South Church in Boston. Such highly distinguished ministers as Pierpont, Palfrey, Ware Sr., Channing, Upham, and Harris, took the several parts. Of these, two only survive, Dr. Palfrey, whom several of us here remember as our teacher in the Theological School, and, remembering, have before us the image of a man as remarkable for method, industry, learning, and accuracy as a teacher, as he was for a conscientious fidelity in the discharge of every duty, the least as well as the greatest; and Charles W. Upham, who had been ordained but a month before, over the First Church in Salem. Mr. Upham, after twenty years in the ministry, retired and became for a time a servant of the country in the National House of Representatives. In his advanced age he has pursued his favorite historical studies, and has, as you know, recently published a Life of Timothy Pickering in four volumes, which has been received with great favor by the public.

The week following the ordination of Dr. Young, came that of the Rev. Edmund Q. Sewall, at Amherst, New Hampshire, a man of rare abilities and virtues; no longer living. At this ordination we find our friend Palfrey taking part with Pierpont, Lowell, and Thayer of Lancaster. This was followed the next week, February 2d, by the ordination of Rev. John Flagg, of West Roxbury, in the exercises of which we find the names of Palfrey again, the lately deceased Dr. Walker, and Drs. Pierce, Lowell, Gray, and Lamson, all well known by those of us who are far advanced in the journey of life, and all, but the first, now gone on out of sight but not beyond the reach of our affections. The week following Mr. Flagg's, came the ordination of that true man and faithful servant of the Lord Jesus Christ, the Rev. Samuel Barrett over the Chambers Street Church in Boston; a man of clear, strong mind, devoted to his work, exercising his ministry in great patience, in great cheerfulness, with great joy in God and great love for the brotherhood. Then followed in the very next week, February 16th, the installation of the Rev. Henry Coleman in the Barton Square Church, of Salem, at which, among others, Messrs. Frothingham, Pierpont, and Brazer officiated. I ought to mention that at the beginning of the same year, 1825, if not a little earlier, our eminent brother, the Rev. E. B. Hall, a particular friend of Dr. Furness, received a call to the then new parish in Northhampton, which the state of his health did not permit him at once to accept. But the parish would not give him up; and in the August ensuing, his health being partially restored, he became their minister; the venerable Dr. Ware preaching the sermon, and Pierpont, Willard, Lincoln, and Brazer, assisting in other exercises.

Said I not truly that the year which gave Dr. Furness to Philadelphia, was memorable for its ordinations in our denomination? Certainly no other has been so fruitful. And all these eminent brothers ordained, with two or three exceptions, were the coëvals and intimate personal friends of him whom we have come here tonight to honor with the outpourings of our respect, gratitude, and affection.

Now there is one other event relating to our good friend, which I hope it will not seem improper for me to refer to, having been for twenty-seven years of my life a minister in the city where it occurred; a very important event in the history of his singularly happy life. It occurred in the year following his ordination; and it has probably had quite as much to do with his comfort and happiness here as your unfailing kindness and sympathy. The event was of so much importance that it was chronicled in the Salem Gazette in this wise:

"In Salem, August 29th, 1825, by Rev. Mr. Emerson, Rev. William Henry Furness, Philadelphia, to Miss

Annis Pulling Jenks, daughter of the late Mr. John Jenks."

I don't dare to tell all I have heard about the bride, though I think from what you now see, you would find no difficulty in believing it. I refer to the event because of its influence and its long-continued charm; and I hope the few lines from Rogers' "Human Life," with which I close, if I can join them to what I have been saying, will not inappropriately relieve your attention.

> "Across the threshold led,
> And every tear kissed off as soon as shed,
> His house she enters there to be a light
> Shining within when all without is night;
> A guardian angel o'er his life presiding,
> Doubling his pleasures and his cares dividing;
> Winning him back when mingling with the throng,
> Back from a world we love, alas, too long,
> To fireside happiness, to hours of ease,
> Blest with that charm—the certainty to please."

I am requested to introduce our Brother Chadwick, of Brooklyn.

Rev. John W. Chadwick, of Brooklyn, N. Y., spoke as follows:

DEAR FRIENDS: It seems to be the order of the evening for each speaker to justify in some way his presence on this sacred and beautiful occasion, and I, knowing that my turn was coming, have been not a little troubled as to what I should say for myself. But Dr. Thompson has helped me out. In the accounts of various ordinations which he has read to you, you must have noticed how few old men had anything to do with them, from which it would appear that, whether there is or is not less respect for age now than formerly, there was formerly much more respect for young men than at present. Nowadays we never take up with any

young men at ordinations and such times, till there are
no more old men to be had. I suspect, therefore, that I
have been invited to speak here this evening as a sign
that respect for young men has not entirely died out.

Dear friends, I saw this occasion while it was yet a
great way off. When Robert Collyer said to me up at
Saratoga last September, "John, we must all go to
Philadelphia next January," I answered, "I have been
meaning to this three years." After your invitation
came, thinking it might possibly mean that I should say
something, I began to think what I would say, and all at
once I found my thought was going to a sort of tune. I
couldn't account for it except by the fancy that my
thought was sympathizing with the music of Dr. Furness'
life, which has been a sort of symphony—a "Pastoral
Symphony"—for has not the thought of the Good Shep-
herd been the central thought and inspiration of it all
from the beginning until now?

Here is what came to me.

W. H. F.

January 12*th*, 1825.   *January* 12*th*, 1875.

Standing upon the summit of thy years,
  Dear elder brother, what dost thou behold,
Along the way thy tireless feet have come
  From that far day, when young and fresh and bold,
Hearing a voice that called thee from on high,
Thou answeredst, quickly, "Father, here am I."

Fain would we see all that thine eyes behold,
  And yet not all, for there is secret store
Of joy and sorrow in each private heart,
  To which no stranger openeth the door.
But thou canst speak of many things beside,
While we a little space with thee abide.

Tell us of those who fifty years ago
　Started thee forth upon thy sacred quest,
Who all have gone before thee, each alone,
　To seek and find the Islands of the Blest.
To-day, methinks that there as well as here
Is kept all tenderly thy golden year.

Tell us, for thou didst know and love him well,
　Of Channing's face,—of those dilating eyes
That seemed to catch, while he was with us here,
　Glimpses of things beyond the upper skies.
Tell us of that weak voice, which was so strong
To cleave asunder every form of wrong.

Thou hast had good companions on thy way;
　Gannett was with thee in his ardent prime,
And with thee still when outward feebleness
　But made his spirit seem the more sublime,
Till, like another prophet, summoned higher,
He found, like him, a chariot of fire.

And that beloved disciple was thy friend,
　Whose heart was blither than the name he bore,
Who yet could hide the tenderness of May,
　And bleaker than December, downward pour
The tempest of his wrath on slavery's lie,
And all that takes from man's humanity.

And thou hast walked with our Saint Theodore,
　Our warrior-saint, well-named the gift of God,
Whose manful hate of every hateful thing,
　Blossomed with pity, e'en as Aaron's rod,
And lips that cursed the priest and Pharisee
Gathered more honey than the wilding bee.

All these are gone, and Sumner's heart beneath
　Should make more pure the yet untainted snow;
Our one great statesman of these latter days,
　Happy wert thou his other side to know,
To call him friend, whom ages yet unborn
Shall love tenfold for every breath of scorn.

All these are gone, but one is with us still,
   So frail that half we deem she will not die,
But slow exhale her earthly part away,
   And wear e'en here the vesture of the sky.
Lucretia, blessed among women she,
Dear friend of Truth, and Peace, and Liberty.

And one, whose form is as the Son of man,
   Has been with thee through all these busy years,
Holden our eyes, and He to us has seemed
   As one seen dimly through a mist of tears;
But thou hast seen him clearly face to face,
And told us of his sweetness and his grace.

Standing upon the summit of thy years,
   Dear elder brother, thou canst see the day
When slavery's curse had sway in all the land,
   And thou art here, and that has passed away.
We give thee joy that in its hour of pride,
Thy voice and hand were on the weaker side.

But from thy clear and lofty eminence
   Let not thine eyes be ever backward turned,
For thou canst see before as cannot we
   Who have not yet thy point of 'vantage earned.
Tell us of what thou seest in the years
That look so strange, seen through our hopes and fears.

Nothing we know to shake thy steadfast mind;
   Nothing to quench thy heart with doubt or fear;
But higher truth and holier love revealed,
   And justice growing to man's heart more dear.
And everywhere beneath high heaven's cope,
A deeper trust, a larger, better hope.

There are some here that shall not taste of death
   Till they have seen the kingdom come, with power.
O brave forerunner, wheresoe'er thou art,
   Thou wilt be glad with us in that glad hour.
Farewell! Until we somewhere meet again.
We know in whom we have believed. Amen.

Rev. Mr. Chadwick, in turn, introduced the Rev. R. R. Shippen, of Boston, Mass., who said:

MY DEAR FRIENDS: Amid these memorials of your Christmas rejoicing, and these fresh flowers and evergreens of tropical luxuriance with which you would symbolize the fragrance of the memories that cluster round this aniversary, and your desire to keep them green, it is my pleasant privilege to speak for the Unitarian Association a word of greeting, giving you congratulations on this your golden wedding, with best wishes for the coming years. Yet as I speak for the Association, I remember that some of our noblest and best, from Channing through the list, have been somewhat fearful of ecclesiastical entanglements, and of hard, dry machinery, and have deemed the truest and best work in life that wrought by character and personal influence; even as Jesus himself did his work, not by organizations, but by his own personality. Permit me then to touch two or three lines of personal influence flowing forth from this pulpit, that are but representatives of many more. Let me speak for one in your city, now in her ninety-third year, kept from this meeting only by the feebleness of old age, who this afternoon told me of her fresh remembrance of the occasion of fifty years ago, vivid as if but yesterday, who has been a lifelong friend of our cause, a generous worker in this church and benefactor of the Meadville Church and Theological School, who recognizes this pulpit as the source of some of the choicest inspirations of her life. Shall I speak for one who in a large home-circle of many brothers has been a loving, sisterly influence of sweetness and light? who in her youth was here a worshiper, and caught the inspiration of this place, and in her greeting sent me to-day writes that she is with us here in spirit to-night; that no one present can join in these services with a more deep and tender gratitude, and no human thought can fully know what her life owes to the ministry we now commemorate? Shall I speak for another, a younger brother, the brightest of the seven, whose youth and early manhood were spent in this city in study and practice of law? who Sunday by Sunday learned here that blessed faith that, when in the full promise of his manly prime his last hour came, enabled him to go bravely to death full of a cheerful hope of immortality? As to-night he makes heaven more real and more attractive to my thought, in his name I pay the tribute of thanks for the inspirations of this pulpit. Shall I speak for myself? In my early home I remember your pastor's familiar volume of "Family Prayer" as a household word. At the outset of my ministry, at the Portland Convention, just twenty-five years ago, I first heard the genial, charming, gracious word of your minister in his prime. And as in Boston one may, day by day, correct his own timepiece by Cambridge observations of the sky, whose electric communications give us every passing hour the celestial time true to the second, so in my young ministry at Chicago,—a lonelier frontier post then than now,—when the barbarous Fugitive Slave Law passed through Congress, and the Northwest Territories were opened for slavery, and the dark days came upon the nation, if, as I tried, I bore any worthy testimony for freedom, I rejoice that I was aided in setting my conscience true to the celestial time by this observatory in Philadelphia. The blessed influences of your pulpit have run their lines through our land and through the world.

And, friends, what does our Association seek but to extend and multiply these lines of personal influence, to enable Boston and Philadelphia to join hands in the same noble work? When I asked your pastor for the last book of Whittier, that I might quote a forgotten line, he replied, "All good books have feet and wings and will find their way at last." But our Association only desires to quicken their speed, and by the people's generosity to enlarge their wings; that as we are now sending Channing through the land, we should gladly send the noble words of Dewey and Furness flying on the wings of the wind.

And what do our Association and Conferences stand for but for fellowship? for the good-will and helpfulness of brotherly greetings? Pennsylvanian as I am by birth and ancestry, with you I rejoice that these Boston brethren have been brought to Philadelphia. It will do us all good to know more of each other. This meeting to-night is just like our Conferences, where our hearts are warmed by words of brotherly kindness. As I recall your minister's inspiring word at the Portland Convention, it has been one of the regrets of my life that we have not heard him oftener among us. But it is never too late to mend. On behalf of the Association and the Conference I invite our Brother Furness and all of you to attend our meetings henceforth every time.

And now, my friends, when Brother Mumford wrote that editorial last week, I said, "You are a generous fellow; why didn't you keep that to make a speech from?" I am sure I don't know what he is going to say. I am requested to ask him to speak.

Rev. Thomas J. Mumford. Dear Friends: On account of the lateness of the hour I will only say that that *was* my speech. The next speaker will be Brother White, and when I say Brother White, I mean brother just as much as they did in the days of Henry Ware.

Rev. William O. White, of Keene, N. H., then addressed the meeting as follows:

There is one comfort, dear friends, as I thank you at this late hour, for giving me the pleasure of being with you, and that is, that Philadelphia time is a little more generous than the time which I carry in my pocket; but I will not abuse even Philadelphia time. The word that Brother Mumford just mentioned brings up very dear and tender associations with men so closely united in my memory with our friend and brother, Dr. Furness. But I will not carry out the thought that comes to me. I would gladly help along one or two strains that vibrate in our hearts, as the words are spoken, that "the time will come when we shall take a last farewell of death," and that other word of a younger speaker who almost felt, and almost knew that one of the long-departed friends of our Brother Furness was here.

I am glad to feel that I am here, just as some of my younger friends were, because I am the son of a friend of Dr. Furness, a layman whose tastes led him to the study of theology, and who, I think, was more attached to the studies of the ministry than many of us ministers are. I say this, because as soon as I saw Dr. Furness this morning I was greeted as my father's son.

And I would not have spoken here at all at this late hour, but to try to fasten to those one or two sweet thoughts that have been uttered to-night, to which I have alluded, a line of the poet-sculptor "Michael Angelo." He is contemplating the wasting block of marble upon which he is working; the block lessens; lessens, lessens, continually in size; and so the years of our friend's sweet, earnest ministry here, are fast passing away before our eyes. But the great lesson that I have found, as I go back to the time when I remember to have heard Dr. Furness' voice in my father's house, and in the old pulpit in Salem, and as I remember the week that I spent with him more than a score of years ago, and as I recall the tenderness of his voice, in his supplications and his preaching, only last October, the great lesson I have taken with me about him fastens itself to the line which I am now to quote of "Michael Angelo." As the poet and sculptor contemplated the wasting marble, he said:

"The more the marble wastes, the more the statue grows."

So, with our friend, the years are passing away; passing away, soon they must be gone; but the statue grows with tenderness of heart deeper than ever; that sweet voice, rich with varied experience of the joys and sorrows of those friends of his in his flock, year after year, has acquired an added tenderness; and we feel

"The more the marble wastes, the more the statue grows,"

and we can welcome the time when he, or any of us, who try to live in a like spirit of devotion to the Master, shall "take an everlasting farewell of death."

I am requested to call on our friend Brother Putnam, of Brooklyn, New York.

Rev. Dr. A. P. Putnam made the following address:

MY DEAR FRIENDS: I think it must have been for a larger number of years than Brother Chadwick said for himself, that I have been looking forward to this occasion, meaning to be here not with a set speech, as you will very soon see, but because I wished to come and to say from my heart, I thank you, Dr. Furness.

I remember when I was a bookkeeper in Boston, how my elder brother, who was in the divinity school at that time, used to bring me the volumes of Channing, Buckminster, and Ware, and also various pamphlet sermons of Dr. Furness. I recollect well the delight with which I read Dr. Furness' pages, and the gospel of liberty they taught me, and the new revelation they seemed to give me of the Christ. I have been a disciple following far off. Yet I know I have not lost during all these years the strong conviction I had then. It has deepened and deepened from that time until now. I have gathered his pamphlets wherever I could find them, and with not a little zeal I have searched for all his books, many of which are out of print and are not easily to be found, until, some years ago, I completed the whole list, and I cherish them as among the most precious treasures in my library. The argument which he draws from the naturalness, the simplicity and artlessness of the gospel records for their truth, and the uplifting of the curtain so that the Christ may be seen in his higher spiritual beauty! what a debt do we owe him for that. Does he know? can he know? can we tell him how much the members of our churches feel of gratitude and love to him for all that he has done for us in this way? Perhaps in some far off time he may know it more fully; but it is right, dear friends, that we should come together thus and say these words which are uttered here to-night, and before he has gone away tell him how much we do love and honor him, and why it is we do love and honor him, and why it is that we shall always revere and bless him. When I have thought what words have gone forth from that desk in behalf of liberty and right in this land, I have wished that the church might remain just as it is to-night, and that pulpit just as it is for years and generations to come. It speaks a lesson for all; those words abide with us still; they have come home to our hearts, and kindled in our souls new zeal for the truth as it is in Jesus. How many chains they have broken, and oh! what a welcome, in comparison with which these congratulations of the hour are small indeed, is reserved for our venerable father and friend, from the spirits of the ransomed freedmen who have ascended to heaven, and who will greet him there.

Let me say that forty years ago it was, that Dr. Furness preached the installation sermon of the first minister of the church which I represent here; the first society of our faith in Brooklyn. It seems a long, long while indeed. I have been over ten years there myself. Dr. Farley preceded me, and he was there twenty years or more. Mr. Holland was there several years before him; Mr. Barlow several years before Mr. Holland. Dr. Furness preached the installation sermon of Rev. Mr. Barlow, who was the first minister of our faith in Brooklyn, forty years ago the 17th of last September. Of the ministers who took part in the services of that occasion, all except your pastor and my immediate predecessor, who was then of Providence, R. I., have passed away,—William Ware, John Pierpont, Caleb Stetson, E. B. Hall, and others. Nearly ten years later, Dr. Furness was present at a convention held there at the time of the dedication of our church, and preached the closing communion sermon. His is a familiar name with my people, who are all with you here in the spirit, and would join me, I know, in heartily saying, "God bless him and you, and the cause of humanity and righteousness, which is so dear to you."

I am requested to call upon Rev. Mr. Ames to address you.

Rev. C. G. Ames, of Germantown, Pa., said:

As I am one of the younger brethren, and very much at home, I feel that I should deny myself, and take up my cross, and introduce a brother from a distance, especially as you have met to hear from these patriarchal ministers who can offer things which I cannot. But I may boast one advantage; they cannot see Dr. Furness every day. Nor can I speak freely of what I feel; it is too much like being one of the family. I live too near, and can easily be excused. My voice is very frequently heard in this house. With a heart brimming full, I have the painful pleasure, therefore, of holding it down, knowing it will keep.

I will introduce Rev. Dr. Bellows, of New York.

Rev. Dr. Bellows made the following remarks:

I am sure both modesty and discretion would suggest the wisdom of my being taught by my junior and friend, and in releasing you from any further attendance on this interesting service. As for myself, I feel tired as a child with the pleasures of the evening; and I can conceive that you all must be so tired that you would welcome as your best friend him who would permit you to go home and think over all the kind things you have heard here. And yet I think it is a kind of duty to say a word in behalf of my own people and city, and all that great community which I am privileged to represent here. New York speaks to Philadelphia; and to a good many of us in New York, Brother Furness is more than half of Philadelphia. When we think of Philadelphia we think rather of him than of anything else, and it is not for anything he has done either; not for all that great service to freedom, not for all that valuable contribution to theological speculation or criticism, but for being what he cannot possibly help, and that is, himself. It is so much more to be than to say, or even to do, that I have not always a great deal of praise for the bright things he does, or the bright things he says,—only because he is what he is and can't help it, and deserves very little thanks for it; for God is the being we must thank, not him. It is, therefore, that I am by force compelled to thank God for him, and not thank him.

Good fellow! he has had it all himself. God gave him all his precious gifts; he gave him his broad and generous humanity; made him a harp for all the winds of heaven and earth to play on, not a fife, to be stopped; gave him that benignant smile which he doesn't know anything about himself; and gave him that delicious voice which is in itself a harmony of all his sweetest powers, an expression of the depth and clearness of his spirit.

Poor fellow! he cannot help it; he has carried it with him all these seventy-two years. And, surely, the first time I ever saw him his voice was the thing that spoke to me. I didn't care what it said; there it was, and I have often thought if a soft voice be an excellent thing in woman, such a voice as his is, is one of the most magnificent and significant gifts that God ever gives to man. Well, let us thank God for him, and then let us thank him for using those talents so well. Now let me thank you in behalf of the denomination, dear brethren, for not being able to be otherwise than so generous, so kind and faithful to a man who, for all I know, never used one particle of machinery to keep you together, has taken no particular pains to keep you together, but just stood like a kind of magnet, and drawn you to his heart. We don't understand it all, but God does; and we see how with a witchery he has done more than most of us are able to do by getting every sort of instrumentality at work that we can possibly use to supplement the defects of our natural constitution. I wish I could work just as Dr. Furness does, and have that same influence and power, without seeking any. If I could stand up in naked simplicity and majesty, and then win the people without using all this painful labor, this fatiguing desperately drudging machinery, I should be very glad indeed; but for most of us poor fellows, it is a necessity to resort to these matters, to supplement the defects of our natural constitution and faculties; but I think Brother Furness can do without it. One thing further I will say of Dr. Furness. It is a subject of special congratulation that he has been always himself; that no theological or critical studies have given an ecclesiastical tinge or twist to his character, or prevented the people from seeing him in his native outline. He has been a preacher and minister, but still more, a man, and although no man less deserves, in the depreciating sense, the name of a man of the world, yet in a noble sense he has been a man of the world; for he has made the world tributary to his growth; drawn in its widest culture, enjoyed its largest freedom, entered into its everyday feelings and joys, and made it his own by his great enjoyment of it, and insight into its meaning. Neither ecclesiasticism nor dogmatism has been able to quench his native originality, and that is one of his chief charms to-day.

Dear brethren, let me congratulate you at the close of this half century of your minister's labors, upon what we now behold in the magnificent development of the theological ideas and religious temper for which our branch of the church has meanwhile stood. We expected great things, but we have seen larger ones, although of a different kind. We looked for a multiplication of our churches, which we have not seen, but how vast has been the spread of our ideas and principles? We expected to be the chief instruments in the work of liberalizing Christian thought and feeling, but Divine providence took up the work with larger methods and new agencies, and made us rather sharers than leaders in theological reform. We happened to be the first wave of what turned out to be an incoming tide, which has swept the whole church on. I think Luther did not see in his day a greater, a more important reformation in theological ideas than we have realized in the last half century.

Whether there be one Unitarian church in Philadelphia or more, or whether our churches in New York and Brooklyn, Baltimore and Washington, New England and the West have multiplied as fast as we hoped or not, there is more liberal Christianity preached in this country to-day, than the boldest prophets could have foreseen when our enterprise started. It has advanced, and it has triumphed, by whatever way. God has taken it up, and brought the aid of a broad science, a broad philosophy, a broad reformatory influence in society, during all these last years, to bear powerfully upon it. We have seen results which may cause many of us to say, "Mine eyes have seen thy salvation; let now thy servant depart in peace." I feel no further anxiety about the spread of liberal Christianity. It now spreads by a necessity. It is a glorious privilege to work in it and for it. But the business is essentially done. The leaven is at work, and it is working everywhere, just as much in the orthodox churches, so-called, as in our own. And very little free thinking is done in our denomination which is not just as fully represented in the old orthodoxy. We are no longer the sole officers in that great army. I thank God that the business of fighting is pretty much over, and that we are now beginning to think more of cultivating religiously the area which has been left for us specially to take care of. Let us now look to it, as churches and ministers and parishes, and see that we produce workmen, and, finally, spiritual fruit, in the particular area over which we are set as husbandmen and gardeners. That you may succeed in cultivating your own soil, and in making the vineyard a nobler and grander one, and in bringing forth more clusters of grapes of the particular vine from which you are set, is my earnest prayer. And that we may all return from these services bearing your blessings and Brother Furness' blessing with us into our own several fields of labor, and that we may be abler and nobler and more careful shepherds, and more faithful husbandmen, is the best thing I can ask, that we may be permitted to carry away from this hour and this blessed assembly of Unitarian Christians and friends.

Music.

Duet for Two Sopranos and Chorus, . . MENDELSSOHN.
"I waited for the Lord," from "Hymn of Praise."
Chorus, ... SPOHR.
"Happy who in Thy House Reside."

Dr. Furness then addressed the meeting.

DEAR FRIENDS: While I am very glad to meet here my brothers in the ministry, and am not at all insensible to their kind words, I call you all to witness that they are not here by my invitation. I never invited them to come here and talk about me. But as long as they have done so, I congratulate you all, and all who are interested in the success of the good cause. It is, you see, in the hands of young men. Although some of your guests here show gray on their heads, they are very young men evidently, fond, especially brother Bellows, of romancing. I use the words that Dr. Bancroft used at my ordination: "It was a comfort to him to feel that as he was going away the cause would be left in hands that would carry it on a great deal better than he could." Some of my friends told me I had better not come here to-night; but brother Bellows intimated to me that by staying away I might seem to be bidding for praise. So I thought I would come and see whether some restraint could not be put upon the speakers by my presence. But I don't think I have availed much.

The day that I was ordained—but I am not going to tire you with old time stories,—when an old minister begins telling his experiences we never know when he will stop—we were all invited,—the gentlemen of the clergy, and the delegates from Boston and New York,—to dine at Mr. Thomas Astley's, who lived at the corner of Ninth and Walnut Streets, a wealthy Englishman of our persuasion. While we were sitting waiting for dinner, the report came that the kitchen chimney was on fire! One of the gentlemen suggested that the fire could be put out very readily by putting a blanket before the chimney, and throwing some sulphur into the fire-place. After dinner, when the wine was passed around and the toasts were given, one of the gentlemen proposed " the *Furnace* that had been kindled in Philadelphia." And another added, "May it never be put out with brimstone."

The meeting was closed by a benediction pronounced by Dr. Furness.

LETTERS.

THE FOLLOWING LETTERS WERE RECEIVED BY
THE COMMITTEE FROM PERSONS WHO
WERE UNABLE TO BE PRESENT.

SHEFFIELD, January 4th, 1875.

TO THE COMMITTEE OF THE FIRST CONGREGATIONAL SOCIETY OF UNITARIANS.

GENTLEMEN: I am obliged and gratified by the invitation. I wish that I could comply with it. It would have been a great pleasure to me, to join the friends of your honored pastor, in commemorating a ministry, not only so long, but otherwise equally remarkable. I should like to be in your church on that interesting evening of the 12th, to hear the pleasant things that will be said, and to say some, perhaps, myself.

But I cannot, that is, I cannot take so long a winter journey. I am not sure enough of my health and strength to venture upon it. Will you give my love to Dr. Furness and his family, and accept for yourselves and the society, the congratulations with which I am,

Very truly yours,
ORVILLE DEWEY.

HAZELWOOD, CAMBRIDGE, January 6th, 1875.

GENTLEMEN: I feel very much honored and gratified by your invitation to be present at the commemoration of Dr. Furness' settlement in the ministry in Philadelphia, but the state of my health forbids me to accept the invitation. My interest in your society dates from a still earlier period.

I have listened in your old Octagon Church to the preaching of Mr. Taylor, and I believe of Mr. Vaughan, as well as preached there repeatedly myself. For more than fifty years I have been your pastor's admirer and warm friend.

I heartily wish him future happy years of earthly life, and I pray God that after his retirement from your service another pastor may serve you with an ability and zeal not too inferior to his.

I am, gentlemen,
Very respectfully,
Your obedient servant,
JOHN G. PALFREY.

CAMBRIDGE, January 1st, 1875.

GENTLEMEN: I regret very sincerely that college duties render it impossible for me to accept your invitation. Regarding your pastor with equal reverence and affection, I should deem it a great privilege to be present at the commemorative services, from which imperative necessity alone would detain me.

I am, gentlemen,
Very truly yours,
A. P. PEABODY.

HINGHAM, January 4th, 1875.

GENTLEMEN: I thank my dear friend, Dr. Furness, and the committee for thinking of me at this time. I should be so very happy to be with you, and join in all the expressions of respect and love for one whose long and faithful ministry has earned the esteem and confidence of all who know him. Beside this, Dr. Furness and I alone continue in the ministry, of those who were classmates in the Divinity School and, I think, in College. Give my love to your pastor. I need not wish him a happy old age. That blessing is assured to him by his fidelity to his convictions of truth and duty through life.

Very respectfully,
CALVIN LINCOLN.

CAMBRIDGE, January 5th, 1875.

GENTLEMEN: I received your invitation to be present at the observance of the fiftieth anniversary of the settlement of your pastor, Dr. Furness. It would give me great pleasure to attend. But I do not feel at liberty to be absent from my regular duty so long as would be required.

No occasion of the kind so significant has occurred for many years. For fifty years Dr. Furness has stood at his post, and manfully defended the cause of what he deemed Divine Truth and Divine Right. He has never failed to hold up the highest standard of private and public duty. He has made no abatement from the truth in his utterance of it, nor deformed it by an immoral spirit. For fifty years he has been an untiring student of the life of Jesus Christ in the four gospels, seeking to bring to light the reality of that life, the internal evidence of the truthfulness of the original record of it, and the moral grandeur and spiritual beauty of the life itself. He has followed in no servile spirit, but with original force of thought, his great teacher, Mr. Norton, from whom, differing in many things, he caught the impulse to this line of inquiry, this work of love, in which his merit has been unique, his service one never to be forgotten. To this it may be added, with universal consent, that his living example has been in harmony with the great subject of his studies, and has done as much as that of any minister to show the worth of the office of spiritual instructor to a generation too ready to distrust those who exercise it. Though not many years younger, I have the habit of looking up to him, and he is one of those from whom inspiration and strength have flowed into my soul when most needed.

I am, brethren, yours in Christian fellowship, with thanks for your kind invitation, and full sympathy with you in all that belongs to a most memorable occasion.

OLIVER STEARNS.

ROXBURY, MASS., January 7th, 1875.

DEAR SIRS: I very much regret that the state of my health forbids my being present at the commemoration, not of the close, thank God! but of the close of the first fifty years of the ministry of Dr. Furness. I regret it not only on account of my personal affection for the minister, but because it has been a ministry eminently after my own heart, one that I admire exceedingly. What I know of it is derived only from glimpses and intuitions, and will be filled out and corrected by the fuller face-to-face knowledge of the parishioners. It has looked to me at this distance as a ministry of a mild and quiet type, as of one that doth not strive nor cry, neither doth any man hear his voice in the streets. Other ministries have been more effective as the multitude measures efficiency, dealing with larger crowds, using more complex agencies, and touching society at more numerous points of interest and with intenser action; but within its own sphere it has dealt with a profoundness and fidelity not elsewhere surpassed with the soul's greatest interests, uncompromising in its absolute loyalty to truth and right, always taking the highest ground, always elevated and elevating, always searching, quickening, soothing, sanctifying to heart and conscience, a lifelong dispensary of Sermons from the Mount.

The specialty of this ministry, it seems to me, has been the unfolding of the personality and character of Jesus of Nazareth. I do not believe there is a pulpit in Christendom that has done so much to penetrate the heart and life of the Master to its inmost depths, and open its riches to the sympathies and acceptance of men, as that Philadelphia pulpit for the last fifty years. Every shade and turn of thought, every gleam of emotion heavenward and earthward, all the sweet humanity and grand divinity of that wonderful soul, have been discerned and delineated there as never elsewhere, I think, and dwelt on with all the earnest zeal and affectionate faith of a disciple, and all the enthusiastic appreciation of an artist—dwelt on almost too exclusively one might think, were it not done by one who knew how to draw all living waters from that one well, and bring up all the gold and gems of the moral and spiritual universe from that one mine. I have no doubt this has been done in this case, so far as any single mind can be comprehensive and all-sided enough to do it.

The ministry which you commemorate has been singularly *self-contained*, that is, has been carried on apart from all official and organic connection with other ministries, without denominational bonds, with no outside ties except those of a fraternal and genial spirit. I sympathize with the characteristics of Dr. Furness' ministry; my own has been conducted on a similar plan, though I fear with less fixedness of principle, and less consistency of action. Most of our brethren will call this our fault, our limitation. Well, they are the majority, and must decide that point; only I am sure they will have the charity to own that we, being such as we are, could do no otherwise.

You of Philadelphia do not need reminding; but I want to express my own appreciation of the manner in which the ministry you celebrate has all along been adorned, refined, deepened, and broadened by literary studies and artistic taste and culture, bringing to that ministry contributions, or rather an aroma and innumerable subtle and sweet influences from all realms of spiritual beauty and fragrance and sunshine.

Shall I dare in such a letter as this to make allusion to the way that looks to me so felicitous, in which the church in the sanctuary has been supplemented by "the church in the house?" To my eye and my remembrance the home in Pine Street, and the church on Locust and Tenth, in the hospitable, genial, cheerful, affectionate, and ever gracious spirit that pervaded them both, were always the counterparts and archetypes of one another, each reflecting what was best and brightest and holiest in the other.

Though this long ministry has been characteristically so quiet and even and suave, it has had epochs and aspects, or one at least, of the kind, in presence of which the earth is shaken, and principalities and powers are prostrated. We may have doubted the wisdom and necessity of the course taken by our brother; but we cannot fail to recognize the sublime moral grandeur of clear and strong convictions adhered to and acted on, with immovable persistence, at all risks and at all cost, and though the heavens fall. We should be blind not to discern there the stuff of which martyrs were made, and the spirit that bore the meek and gentle Jesus to his cross.

Perhaps my mind has dwelt more on the jubilee from the fact that if all had gone well with me, I should have been the next among the liberal ministers, so far as I know, to have been entitled to such an occasion for myself. I have had my nine lustra, and if the tenth fail why should I complain? I can still rejoice with all my heart in the well-earned honors and happiness of my well-beloved friend and brother in Philadelphia.

Very truly yours,
GEORGE PUTNAM.

106 MARLBOROUGH STREET,
BOSTON, January 4th, 1875.

DEAR SIRS: I am deeply indebted to you for the very kind invitation to be present at the fiftieth anniversary of Dr. Furness' settlement. I regret to say that I cannot leave my work at that time.

I am sure that you have reason to thank God and take courage as you look back upon the half century. Dr. Furness has served nobly both in Church and State, and has done much to show that the two are indeed one. My warmest wishes accompany him as he enters upon his green old age, which surely lacks nothing that should go along with it. May he have the outward strength, as he is sure to have the inward desire, to speak to you and for you these many years.

Gratefully and sincerely yours,
RUFUS ELLIS.

PORTLAND, MAINE, January 4th, 1875.

It is with great regret that I find myself unable to accept your kind invitation to be present at the fiftieth anniversary of the settlement of the Rev. Dr. Furness.

During the whole of that fifty years, and it embraces all my life excepting the seven years of infancy, I have had near relations and friends among the parishioners and lovers of Dr. Furness, so that my interest in the occasion is almost personal. But I am obliged to be in Philadelphia a fortnight later, and cannot possibly spare the time for both journeys.

With the most cordial congratulations for both pastor and people, and the hope of many happy returns of the season, I remain,

Very respectfully and truly yours,
THOMAS HILL.

CAMBRIDGE, MASS., January 2d, 1875.

GENTLEMEN: I am very sorry that I cannot accept your kind invitation to be present at the fiftieth anniversary of the settlement of Dr. Furness as your minister.

The fact of so long a pastorship is itself noteworthy in these days of change; but, in this case, we have all a special right to be sharers in your joy, since we have received our part in the fruit of your minister's labors during these fifty years. Dr. Furness has set an example, rare in these days of divided and superficial work, not only by his devotion to a single parish during so long a period, but also by his consecration to one chosen line of thought. He selected the noblest theme and gave his life to it, and made us all his debtors. With thanks for your kind invitation, and congratulations for minister and people,

I am, yours very truly,
C. C. EVERETT.

BOSTON, January 9th, 1875.

GENTLEMEN: Since I heard that your jubilee was proposed I have hoped to be able to be present, but I am, at the last moment, disappointed. I think our friends in Philadelphia must understand that they are only a very small part of the multitude of people who are grateful to Dr. Furness for the labors and the love of his wonderful life. So soon as we who were then youngsters found out how he preached, we used to say we would walk fifty miles barefoot to hear him, if there were no other way to enjoy that privilege. But even more than the preaching, it was the reading of the books, and the living picture which they gave us of the Saviour's life, that set us on a track of preaching and of thought wholly new.

Let me congratulate the congregation on his health and strength, and pray express for a multitude of us our love and gratitude to him.

Truly yours,
EDWARD E. HALE.

DORCHESTER, MASS., January 10th, 1875.

GENTLEMEN: I have delayed replying to your letter of invitation to be present with you on the 12th instant, because, while my very earnest desire was to accept it, and my heart spontaneously said "yes," there were circumstances making it questionable whether I could. Those circumstances, I am sorry to have now to say, have decided for me that I must deny myself the hoped-for pleasure.

I can do no less, gentlemen, than express to you, and those for whom you act, my sincere thanks for this thought of me in such connection, and for including me among the friends of your minister who were considered worthy to be gathered around him on such an occasion.

Though I can hardly believe that my presence would add anything to the enjoyment of it, I think no one will enter more heartily than I should into all that belongs to it for memory and sentiment and affection and benediction.

Your minister seems very near to me as he is very dear. My acquaintance with him dates back to his boyhood. He is most intimately associated in memory, as he was in fact, with those nearest to me of my early home, whose love for him I shared;

a love joined with admiration for his dispositions and gifts. They are all gone to whom I allude; and the more tenderly for that does my heart, as it bearing their love with its own, embrace him and this occasion.

And the feelings inspired by those earlier memories towards him whom in this occasion you so deservedly honor have been, I hardly need say, continually deepening, as I have followed him through his life since, and seen the promise our hearts cherished in him unfold towards a fulfillment so beautiful and rich.

Most heartily do I congratulate the members of his society in the privilege they have enjoyed in him whose very presence has been a benediction, and whose life, in its simplicity and sanctity and humble heroism and self-devoting fidelity, has given such empowerment to his words, and won for them such place in many hearts beyond those who have been the immediate recipients of them.

Much more is in my heart to say, less I could not, in justice to myself, and as a fitting response (the most so in my power to make) to your very kind invitation.

If I may be allowed to add what is so wholly personal to myself, I would say that the memories which connect myself with your church as being the first I ever preached in, forty-one years ago, and the memories of those of it who so kindly received me (so many of whom have passed away), have deepened my desire towards an occasion of such varied and touching interest. With the prayer that heaven's blessing may rest upon minister and people,

I am, respectfully yours,
NATHANIEL HALL.

BALTIMORE, MD., January 9th, 1873.

Very many thanks for your kind invitation. I have a wedding on the night of January 15th, which I fear, as I have not, so far, been able to postpone or advance, will prevent my going to Philadelphia. I have not given up all hope yet. I wish to assure you of the great pleasure I would take in witnessing the celebration of an event so marked in our common history, and so full of inspiration to a young man like myself, and I hope that beautiful life which has so blessed you through these years,

may be spared to repeat, in your midst, that old story, which he has made so living, of God's great mercy and love made real in the divine life on earth. With greetings and congratulations,
I am most truly,
C. R. WELD.

St. Louis, January 4th, 1875.

DEAR SIRS: Your kind invitation to be present at the commemoration of the fiftieth anniversary of Dr. Furness' settlement in Philadelphia was to-day received, and I wish for my own sake that I could accept it. But my engagements here are such as to make it impossible for me to leave St. Louis, and I must be content to stay at home. Dr. Furness was one of my earliest friends and guides, to whom I have always looked up with sincere affection and respect. He officiated at my marriage with the best woman that ever lived, and I associate him with all the purest happiness and success of my own life.

William Henry Furness: For fifty years of faithful service, the brave and consistent advocate, in good report and evil report, of Freedom, Truth, and Righteousness: May his last days still be his best days.
I remain, very truly yours,
W. G. ELIOT.

Chicago, January 26th, 1875.

GENTLEMEN: When you sent me an invitation to be present at the fiftieth anniversary of the settlement of my dear friend and yours, I felt sure I should be able to come. My youngest boy had been sick then for some weeks, so that I could only leave him a few hours at a time, and for the most imperious reasons. But on the Saturday he was so much worse that I had to telegraph I feared I could not leave him at that time.

There can be but few reasons in a man's whole lifetime so strong as mine was then for coming to Philadelphia, but the poor little fellow begged I would be with him through a very dangerous operation the surgeons had to perform on the day I should have been with you, from which we were not sure he could rally.

Pardon me for touching with this private sorrow your exceeding joy, and accept this for my reason why I have not written sooner.

I did not want to intrude these things at all even into the blessed after-taste of your festival. But as it seems to me no man on the earth could be so strongly drawn to that festival as I was, from any distance, I cannot say another word until you know the whole reason why I was not with you.

For my debt of gratitude to Dr. Furness takes precedence of my love for him as one of the truest friends a man ever had, and as my peerless preacher of "the truth as it is in Jesus," some years before I emigrated to America, my soul clove to him as I sat one day in a little thatched cottage in the heart of Yorkshire and read "The Journal of a Poor Vicar."

I never expected to see him in the flesh then, but I remember how I cherished that exquisite little thing among my choicest treasures; read it over and over again; spoke of it to other lads of a like mind with my own, and got a worth out of it I had not then begun to get out of sermons.

I knew also, when I got to Philadelphia, that I could hear my man preach if I wanted to, and made out where the church was; but I had been taught from my childhood to give such churches a wide berth, and had not the sense to see that the well, out of which I had drawn such sweet waters in England, must still be flowing with some such blessing in America. So that mighty movement that ended in breaking the fetters from the slave, had to break mine, and then it was not very long before I stole into the church one dismal Sunday night, when being good Unitarians, all but about a dozen of you, you had your feet in slippers on the fender.

It was not a sermon, but a talk about Jesus; and how he washed their feet, and what they saw, and what he said, and how it all came home to the preacher; but as I went home I thought, as so many have done time and time again, if that is Unitarianism I am a Unitarian.

When again I met my author and preacher at the house of my friend, Edward M. Davis, it did not take long for my gratitude to grow into love. He was positively the first minister of the sort we call "ministers in good standing," except Mrs. Lucretia Mott, who had not tried to patronize me, and put up the bars of a superior social station.

If I had been his younger brother, he could not have been

more frank and tender and free of heart and hand. I suppose he never thought of it for an instant, and that was where he had me, or I should have put up my bars. For, in those days, I guess I was about as proud as Lucifer. So, it was a great pride and joy in 1857, to be invited to preach in his pulpit, while he went off to marry another son in the faith, Moncure D. Conway, to be the guest, for that day, of your minister's family, to have Mrs. Furness and the children treat me like a prince and a preacher all in one, and to have a glorious good time altogether, as any man ever had in this world.

Being good Unitarians again in those days, at least half of you ran off to hear Brother Chapin in the morning, who was preaching somewhere round the corner, just as my people run now to hear Brother Swing when I am away, and have to supply with some man they never heard of. I have never quite forgiven Chapin for preaching there that Sunday.

But Annie Morrison was there, and the very elect, who are always there, and on the next Sunday, when I preached again, the rest were there, and the glory of the Lord seemed to me to fill the house, and so your church is to me one of the most precious places on earth. I came to it as the men of Israel went to Zion, and all these years have but deepened and purified my love for the good old place. Where I first heard the truth which met at once my reason and my faith, and where, within a church, for the first time I felt I was perfectly free.

And so it is, that I dare not write down the sum of my love for my friend and his family, as I could not have told it if I had come down. I feel I am under bonds not to do it; I can only hint at it.

He got used to blame in the old sad days, when he could not count such hosts of lovers and friends outside his own church as he can now, but he will never get used to praise. Some men don't. I must say, however, that I do not see how I should ever have made my way into our blessed faith, had he not opened the door for me; or found my way to Chicago but for his faith that I was the man they wanted here; or done anything I have ever been able to do half so well, but for his generous encouragement, or found my life at all so full of sunshine, as it has been so many years, had he not given me of his store.

Now and then, the ways of God do visibly strike great harmonies in life and history, and this perfecting of the circle of fifty years in the ministry of my dear friend, is one of the harmonies of life. He has seen the travail of his soul for the slave, and is satisfied.

He has lived through the days when the majority of Unitarians were content with being not very unlike the Orthodox, into the days when the Orthodox are not content, if they are not very like Unitarians, and he has done one of the heaviest strokes of work in bringing this resolution about.

And he has lived to prove to those of us who may wonder sometimes, what is coming when we have preached to our people a few more years; and it gets to be an old story, how a man may preach right along, just as long as he can stand, and then sit down to it as Jesus did on the Mount; grow better all the time; win a wider and truer hearing at the end of fifty years than he has at the end of twenty-five; and then, when he is " quite worn out with age," may cry, " Lord, now lettest thy servant depart in peace according to thy word, for mine eyes have seen thy salvation."

Surely yours,
ROBERT COLLYER.

The following extracts are taken from the *Liberal Christian* and *Christian Register*:

"On Tuesday of next week, January 12th, there will be a very simple celebration of a deeply interesting occasion. It will then be fifty years since Rev. Dr. Furness was installed as pastor of the First Congregational Unitarian Church in Philadelphia. Next Sunday the venerable pastor will deliver an appropriate discourse. Tuesday he will receive callers at his house, and in the evening there will be a meeting at the church. Brief addresses are expected from friends, whose homes are in Missouri, Illinois, Maryland, New York, and New England.

"At the installation on the 12th of January, 1825, Rev. William Ware, of New York, aged twenty-seven years, offered the introductory prayer and read from the Scriptures; Rev. Henry Ware, Jr., of Boston, aged thirty years, preached the sermon, most of which we intend to reprint next week; Rev. Dr. Bancroft, of Worcester, in his seventieth year, offered the ordaining prayer and gave the charge; and Rev. Ezra S. Gannett, aged twenty-three years, gave the fellowship of the churches and offered the concluding prayer. Dr. Furness himself was twenty-two years old, having been graduated at Harvard College when he was only eighteen. None of those who took the prominent parts in the service are now living on earth. Dr. Gannett and the Wares, though then in all the strength and promise of their early manhood, have followed good old Dr. Bancroft to the heavenly home.

"Dr. Furness was installed a few weeks before the ordinations of Rev. Drs. Alexander Young and Samuel Barrett. The services were reported in the first number of the second volume of the *Christian Examiner*, and in the fourth volume of the *Christian Register*. It was four months before the organization of the American Unitarian Association. James Monroe was President of the United States. Boston had been a city only three years, and had about fifty thousand inhabitants; New York had about a hundred and sixty thousand, and Philadelphia about a hundred and forty thousand. It was the same year in which the first public railway in England was opened, the passengers being drawn by horse-power, although locomotives were soon introduced. It was five years before Dr. Putnam's settlement in Roxbury, nine years before Dr. Lothrop was called to Brattle Square, ten years before Rev. N. Hall became junior pastor of the Dorchester First Parish, and twelve years before Dr. Bartol became Dr. Lowell's colleague. Dr. Bellows, aged ten years, and James Freeman Clarke, fourteen, were school-boys. Rev. E. E. Hale was scarcely old enough to go to school, and Prof. C. C. Everett had not been born. It was less than half a century since the battles of Lexington and Concord, and Thomas Jefferson and John Adams did not die until eighteen months afterwards. President Grant was then two years old.

"During the whole of the last half century Dr. Furness has remained faithfully at his lonely post. He has had no colleague and no very long vacation, we believe. In addition to his pulpit work he has written some admirable books, besides translating others. Great changes have occurred in public opinion. Eight years after the beginning of his ministry in Philadelphia the American Antislavery Society was formed in that city. He did not join it immediately, but before long he enlisted in the ranks of the abolitionists, and neither blandishments nor threats ever caused him to desert from the forlorn hope of freedom. For many years, when almost every other pulpit of that great town, so near the borders of Slave States, was dumb concerning the national sin, Dr. Furness' silver trumpet gave no uncertain sound. Whoever might come, and whoever might go, he was resolved to be faithful to the slave. The despised and rejected champions of liberty were always sure of his support. When Charles Sumner, struck down by the bludgeon of the slave power, needed rest and healing, he sought them in the neighborhood and society of Dr. Furness. Together they visited the hill country, and mingled their congenial spirits in high discourse of truth and righteousness. We are glad that at last, with grateful ears, our venerated brother heard liberty proclaimed throughout all the land to all the inhabitants thereof. To know that he contributed to this blessed result must be the grand satisfaction of his life, more precious than any pride of authorship or professional success. His whole soul must respond to Whittier's declaration that he set a higher value to his name as appended to an early antislavery declaration than on the title-page of any book. 'I cannot be sufficiently thankful to the Divine Providence which turned me so early away from what Roger Williams calls "the world's great trinity, pleasure, profit and honor," to take side with the poor and oppressed. Looking over a life marked by many errors and shortcomings, I rejoice that

> "'My voice, though not the loudest, has been heard
> Wherever Freedom raised her cry of pain.'

"But while Dr. Furness must look back with profoundest gratitude upon the great triumph of justice which he helped to secure, he cannot be indifferent to the theological progress which has led to wide and cordial acceptance of many of his dearest opinions. Once he was one of a small number of Humanitarians associated with a great majority of Arians. Now the Arians are nearly extinct, and the divine humanity of Jesus is almost orthodox Unitarianism. No other individual has done more to bring this about than the Philadelphia pastor who has made it the study of his life to understand the spirit and to portray, in glowing yet truthful tints, the matchless character of the Son of man. He has been well entitled 'the Fifth Evangelist.' None of the ancient narrators ever lingered so fondly over every trait of him who was touched with a feeling of our infirmities, and made perfect through suffering. He has rendered the sympathy of Christ so actual and available that it is a familiar help to thousands of tried and lonely human souls, to whom traditional dogmas could give no comfort or strength.

"We have heard that Dr. Furness is about to retire from the professional responsibilities which he has borne so long and so well. It will be a richly earned repose, and yet we cannot endure the thought that he is to desist wholly from preaching while his eye is undimmed and his natural vigor scarcely abated. We heard him last summer with rare satisfaction and delight, and we wish he could be induced to speak oftener at our general gatherings. We have thought a great many times, and perhaps we have said so before, in these columns, that, owing largely to force of circumstances, Dr. Furness has borne too close a resemblance to Wordsworth's Milton whose 'soul was like a star, and dwelt apart.' It is too late now for him to be in the slightest danger of becoming too social or gregarious. We wish, most heartily, that he would sometimes meet with the thousands of our laymen and the hundreds of our ministers

to whom he is personally a stranger, never seen, and never heard, and yet they regard him with affectionate gratitude and veneration which it would do them good to express, and not harm him in the least to receive. Let us fondly hope, then, that at the semi-centennial celebration of the American Unitarian Association, or at the next National Conference, we may hear from this beloved father in our Israel some of those words of wisdom, truth, and beauty which it is still his mission to speak."
—*Christian Register.*

"PHILADELPHIA, January 12th, 1875.

"It is safe to predict that not even the powerful attractions of the National Centennial Exposition will call to this city as many of our Unitarian clergy as gathered here to-night to celebrate the semi-centennial of the settlement of Dr. William H. Furness. It is an event to which for some time past many of his absent friends have looked eagerly forward in anticipation of its peculiar interest and significance. Pastorates of fifty years can never be common, and have rarely furnished the necessary materials for the heartiest and sincerest sort of congratulation. But here was an occasion of which the anticipations were all of the pleasantest and most unclouded kind, where everybody felt that it would be a personal privilege to say a congratulatory Amen with everybody else, and to say it heartily and sincerely.

"Dr. Furness' quiet but intensely individual ministry in this city of Brotherly Love is too widely known among Unitarians to make any mere mention of the fact at all necessary, but to speak of it at length and justly would be to write a volume; ample materials for which, however, are, we are glad to say, not wanting. But *our* word must be only of the event of to-day.

"The celebration began, we hear, early in the morning at the pastor's house, where he was delightfully surprised by the sweet carols of children's voices. In the afternoon a large concourse of friends went to greet him at his home, where beautiful flowers scented the air and smiling faces vied with each other in the expression of sincere respect and love.

"This evening the old church is beautifully and richly dressed with evergreens. Below the pulpit is a solid mass of rare tropical plants most tastefully arranged, the whole surmounted by baskets of the choicest flowers. The most conspicuous features of the decorations are the significant numbers 1825-1875, worked in small white flowers on either side of the pulpit.

"The old church is full of the Doctor's parishioners and friends, the front seats being occupied by the invited guests from abroad. Among the clergy present we noticed Drs. Lothrop, Morison, Clarke, Bartol, Bellows, Thompson, A. P. Putnam, and Rev. Messrs. White, E. H. Hall, Shippen, Ware, Ames, Israel, Mumford, Gannett, Chadwick, and several others.

"Dr. Furness had protested against his personal participatior. in this elaborate and deliberate feast of Praise, but the timely suggestion that his absence might be interpreted as a quiet 'bid' for unlimited adulation proved too amusing for the equanimity of even *his* modesty, so he came and occupied a retired seat near the door.

"The proceedings were of the simplest and most informal kind—a genuine love-feast, with more fullness of heart than of utterance. Yet there was no lack of pleasant, hearty words. After an anthem, with solo, by the accomplished choir, which seemed to have been augmented and specially drilled for the occasion, the Chairman of the Committee of Arrangements welcomed the guests and assembled company, and asked Dr. Morison to offer prayer. After a soprano solo, the first speech of the evening was made by Rev. J. F. W. Ware, whose father, Henry Ware, had preached Dr. Furness' ordination sermon. Dr. Furness then came forward, bearing two communion cups which had just been received as a token of remembrance from our church in Baltimore. He expressed his pleasure at this expression of affectionate sympathy, referring, incidentally, to the peculiar method of celebrating the communion in his church, bread and wine not being partaken of, but being placed on the table only as symbols of the precious things they stand for.

"William Gannett, whose father gave the right hand of fellowship at Dr. Furness' ordination, said that this was the principal reason for his presence here to-night. His modest, cordial words were followed by others, from Rev. E. H. Hall and Dr. Lothrop. Dr. J. F. Clarke then read an original poem, in which, in strong and eloquent words, he commended Dr. Furness' earnest and persistent efforts to present more clearly to the world the living Jesus as distinguished from the theological or sentimental Christ. Dr. Bartol and Dr. Thompson then added their cordial testimony of appreciation. Mr. Chadwick read a lovely original poem, full of appreciative references to some of Dr. Furness' more distinguished cotemporaries. Messrs. Shippen, Mumford, White, and Ames, each said a few words, and Dr. Bellows finished the sweet symphony of praise with a genial portraiture of Dr. Furness, thanking the Lord that no amount of culture had in any respect weakened the vigorous manhood of his friend, and that God made him just what he is.

"After music, and a benediction by Dr. Furness, the large company separated, evidently deeply pleased by the many hearty testimonies of the evening."—*Liberal Christian.*

" Yesterday morning, at seven o'clock, the pupils of Madame Seiler, an accomplished teacher of music, and author of several excellent text-books, gave a serenade to Dr. Furness and his household. It must have been a delightful surprise to the awakened family when the sweet sounds began to ascend from the hall below, where the singers, according to the *Bulletin*, stood 'candle in hand,' and paid this delicate and welcome compliment, in the good old German style. Between the hours of twelve and six, hundreds of parishioners and friends called to congratulate the honored pastor upon the successful completion of his half century of service. Most of the time the rooms were thronged, and such an array of bright and happy faces is seldom seen. Among the guests who were present during our brief stay we noticed the Doctor's children and grandchildren, Prof. Goodwin, of Harvard University, and Mrs. Eustis, daughter of Rev. Dr. W. E. Channing.

" Last evening there was a driving storm of sleet and rain, but the church was packed again. The floral display was equal to that of Sunday. Among the changes we observed that the large figures '1825' and '1875,' above the pulpit, were made of pure white flowers instead of white and red as before. After prayer by Rev. Dr. Morison, Mr. Henry Winsor, Chairman of the Committee of Arrangements, made a felicitous welcoming and introductory speech.

"The first clerical speaker was Rev. J. F. W. Ware, son and nephew of the young Wares who, fifty years before, had taken prominent parts at the installation service. His remarks were full of the warmest affection for Dr. Furness, and the tenderest allusions to the love cherished for his Philadelphia 'brother' by Henry Ware, Jr. Agreeably to the request of the committee, Mr. Ware asked Rev. W. C. Gannett to follow him. Mr. Gannett's father gave Dr. Furness the right hand of fellowship, and Mr. Gannett had just been reading the manuscript copy of that earnest address, on his way to Philadelphia in the cars. His speech was eminently appropriate and impressive. He was followed by Rev. E. H. Hall, of Worcester, successor of Rev. Dr. Bancroft, who gave the charge at the installation half a century before, and son of Rev. Dr. E. B. Hall, who was Dr. Furness' townsman, friend, classmate, and roommate. After most appreciative mention of the noble labors of our fathers, Mr. Hall spoke eloquently of the peculiar work which each generation has to do for itself and the world. Rev. Drs. Lothrop, Clarke, Bartol, Thompson, A. P. Putnam, and Bellows, and Messrs. Chadwick, Shippen, White, Mumford, and Ames were called upon, and the most of them responded; but we have no space for their remarks this week. Next week we hope to find room for a report, but now we must content ourselves with copying from the *Bulletin* the poems which were read.

"Before quoting them, however, we must not forget to say that Dr. Furness spoke twice in the course of the evening, the first time acknowledging the gift of some communion cups from the church in Baltimore to the church in Philadelphia. It was hard to believe that this graceful and happy speaker, with as fresh a voice as that of the youngest man heard that evening, and saying the brightest and merriest things of the hour, could be the venerable pastor whose semi-centennial we were celebrating; but we presume that there is not the slightest doubt of the fact. And we must also remember to state that among the gifts from parishioners and friends were some elegant mantel ornaments, and the complete and original manuscript of Charles Lamb's 'Dissertation on Roast Pig.' The *Bulletin* says that this unique and interesting present was 'secured as a Christmas gift at a recent sale in London, and handsomely mounted and bound in large folio form.' "—*Christian Register.*

W. H. F.

"THE FIFTIETH ANNIVERSARY."

BY WM. C. GANNETT.

FIFTY times the years have turned
Since the heart within him burned,
With its wistfulness to be
An apostle sent of Thee.

Closely in his Master's tread
Still to follow, till he read,
Tone of voice and look of face,
Print of wound and sign of grace.

Reading there for fifty years,
Pressing after, till the tears
And the smiles would come and go
At the self-same joy and woe—

Sharing with him shouts of "Mad!"
When the bold front to the bad
Bent to pluck the "little ones"
From the feet of fellow-sons—

Sharing in his inner peace,
But *not* sharing the release,
He is with us while the chimes
Ring his "Well done" fifty times.

Listening boys across the field
Pledge a hope *they* may not yield:
Are they listening from the air —
Boys who started with him there?

REV. DR. FURNESS' RESIGNATION.

On Thursday, January 14th, 1875, Dr. Furness sent the following letter to the Society, resigning the charge of the pulpit into their hands—

TO THE MEMBERS OF THE FIRST CONGREGATIONAL CHURCH.

MY VERY DEAR FRIENDS: While the measure of health and strength still granted me demands my most thankful acknowledgments, and while I am inexpressibly grateful for the recent manifestations of your affectionate regard, I am admonished by the ending of fifty years of service as your minister, and by the time of life that I have reached, that only a little while remains to me at the longest. I am moved, therefore, to resign the charge of the pulpit into your hands. How could I have borne it so long but for your patience and steadfast friendship? I recognize a salutary discipline in the necessity which I have been under all these years of weekly preparation for the Sunday service. It is good, as I have learned, for a man to bear the yoke in his youth, and even in middle age; but now, when only a fragment of life remains to me, I would fain be released from that care, which neither time nor custom has rendered any lighter than in my earlier years.

With the surrender of the pulpit you will understand of course that I decline all further pecuniary support. I beg leave respectfully to suggest that for some time to come the pulpit be supplied by settled ministers, so that nothing shall be done hastily in the matter of deciding upon my successor. Moreover, for all other pastoral offices, I shall be at your service, remaining always your devoted friend, and in undying affection,

Your pastor,
W. H. FURNESS.

January 14th, 1875.

AT a meeting of the Society held in the church Saturday evening, January 23d, 1875, it was voted that the following letter should be sent to Dr. Furness, accepting his resignation, and that the Trustees should sign the same on behalf of the Society.

FIRST CONGREGATIONAL UNITARIAN CHURCH.

PHILADELPHIA, January 25th, 1875.

DEAR DR. FURNESS: The members of this Society have received with sorrow your letter of the 14th inst., in which you resign the charge of the pulpit which you have filled so long, with so much ability and so much to their satisfaction.

Although we deeply regret the existence of the circumstances, which in your opinion have made the step necessary, we acknowledge the justice of permitting you to judge freely of the force of the reasons in its favor, which have governed you in coming to your decision; and though we feel it would be a great privilege to us to have the pastoral relation continued through the coming years, during which we fondly hope you may be spared to us, yet we acquiesce in the propriety of promptly acceding to the wish for relief which you have so decidedly expressed both in your letter and verbally to the committee appointed at our meeting on the 19th inst., to ask you to reconsider your action and to withdraw your resignation. It would be ungrateful for us to do otherwise, and would show on our part a want of proper appreciation of the value of your long-continued labors thus to make what must be to you in itself a painful act still more painful.

We cannot fully express in words our thankfulness that the relation between us has remained unbroken through so many years, and that, though the formal tie may now be severed, we are yet permitted to see you face to face, to hear your voice, to press your hand, and to know that you are among us.

For the reasons which you have presented, and because you so earnestly desire it, because it is our wish to do, at whatever loss to ourselves, that which will be most grateful to you, and thus to manifest in the strongest way we can our appreciation of our privileges in the past, and with the hope that for years

to come you may be with us and of us, we regretfully accept your resignation, and remain, on behalf of the Society,
Your affectionate friends,
HENRY WINSOR,
LUCIUS H. WARREN,
DAWES E. FURNESS,
JOSEPH E. RAYMOND,
JOHN SELLERS, JR.,
ENOCH LEWIS,
CHARLES H. COXE,
Trustees.

This letter was read at the meeting of the congregation, held on Saturday evening, January 23d, 1875, was approved, and the Trustees were instructed to sign it on behalf of the Society and forward it to Dr. Furness.
CHARLES H. COXE,
Secretary.

INDEX.

	PAGE
PRELIMINARY MEETINGS,	3
DR. FURNESS' FIFTIETH ANNIVERSARY DISCOURSE,	9
EXTRACT FROM FORTY-NINTH ANNIVERSARY DISCOURSE,	28
COMMEMORATIVE MEETING,	41
Prayer of Rev. John H. Morison, D.D.,	42
Remarks of Rev. J. F. W. Ware,	44
" " Rev. W. C. Gannett,	48
" " Rev. E. H. Hall,	49
" " Rev. S. K. Lothrop, D.D.,	51
" " Rev. J. F. Clarke, D.D.,	55
" " Rev. C. A. Bartol, D.D.,	57
" " Rev. J. F. Thompson, D.D.,	61
" " Rev. J. W. Chadwick,	66
" " Rev. R. R. Shippen,	70
" " Rev. T. J. Mumford,	72
" " Rev. W. O. White,	72
" " Rev. A. P. Putnam, D.D.,	74
" " Rev. C. G. Ames,	76
" " Rev. H. W. Bellows, D.D.,	77
" " Rev. W. H. Furness, D.D.,	81
LETTERS,	83
EXTRACTS FROM THE "LIBERAL CHRISTIAN" AND "CHRISTIAN REGISTER,"	97
POEM, BY W. C. GANNETT,	104
RESIGNATION OF REV. W. H. FURNESS, D.D.,	105
LETTER OF THE TRUSTEES,	109

www.ingramcontent.com/pod-product-compliance
Lightning Source LLC
Chambersburg PA
CBHW031402160426
43196CB00007B/857